To Chris,

Have a slice of Texas history —

Enjoy,

Buddy

Blessings from the Good Earth

Blessings from the Good Earth

A Young Boy's Story of the Depression in Gonzales, Texas

Buddy Schrader

Published by

The Good Earth Press
PO Box 9091
Horseshoe Bay, TX 78657

Library of Congress Cataloging-in-Publication Data

Schrader, Buddy.
Blessings from the Good Earth

p. c.m. i

1. Schrader—Family History. @. Texas—Family—History.
3. United States—Biography. 4. Family—Texas—Gonzales.
5. Depression—Texas—History. 6. Town life—Texas.

I. Title. II. Authors. III. History. IV. Monograph.

ISBN: 0-9762313-0-1

976.4Sc PS 3561 A6929s

To my parents,

Gladys and Charlie Schrader,

the driving force in my life.

They ran a home of high standards.

Acknowledgments

"Enjoy success," my dad would say, "but be aware that arrogance can sneak up on you." I've had many opportunities to reflect on his advice, particularly in creating this book. I know how success can make you take yourself too seriously and how easy it is to forget those who helped you get where you are. With that in mind, I extend my thanks to the many people who helped me in this endeavor.

First to my wife, Barbara—my sweetheart, counselor, adviser and friend. She gave me the idea, then motivated me, kept me on course and kept me organized. Her talent as an English major helped make this all possible.

Brother Clif, just as big brothers should be, was a wonderful role model during my formative years. He was an indispensable contributor to this book, providing facts and stirring memories that lay deeply buried.

Virgie Van Kleef, my special big sister, provided me with facts, details, pictures and reminders of how great life was in our early years.

Retired Major General Sam Turk, my lifelong friend and schoolmate, made the World War II chapter possible.

Sergeant Sonny Tuch, a poster boy for the "Greatest Generation," shared his stories about fighting with his buddies in Company K. It is an honor to know him.

Alan Winters, one of my high school coaches—and now my golf partner, reminded me how football directed my competitive drive in a positive way.

Velma Marek, eighty-five years young, Mom's friend and quilting partner, is an expert historian for the First Evangelical Lutheran Church of Gonzales. She shared her clear recollection of events sixty years ago.

Dr. Cecil Knox, a dedicated country doctor for fifty years, refreshed my memory of how doctors in Gonzales, with their passion for giving and healing, improved our quality of life.

Robert and Mary Torres, owners of Illusions Photography of Gonzales, provided their photographic expertise.

Billy Lapham of Horseshoe Bay shared his memories of the Depression and reminded me how good life was during those trying times.

Cousins Kathy Vackar, Barbara Harsch and Lynda Evans gathered information, letters and pictures and shared many warm memories.

Barbara A. Langham of Austin, book author, excellent editor and a true professional, edited my first draft and, as a bonus, added fun to the project.

I extend my special appreciation to the following: the Texas Military Forces Museum in Austin, the Gonzales County Chapter of the Texas Extension Homemakers Association, the Gonzales County Courthouse Archives and the Gonzales Chamber of Commerce.

Contents

GONZALES, TEXAS

I was born on a farm south of Gonzales, Texas, in June 1936. That year Franklin Delano Roosevelt, who had become widely popular for creating programs to lift the country out of the Depression, was running for reelection. In Germany, the homeland of my father's ancestors, Adolph Hitler was building an army.

Texas was celebrating the hundredth anniversary of its independence. People from all over the state were traveling to the Texas Centennial Exposition in Dallas that summer, and many small towns were holding celebrations of their own. Gonzales had actually started off the celebrations with its own observance the previous November.

As I would learn years later in my seventh-grade Texas history class, Gonzales was where the first shots were fired in the Texas Revolution. In October 1835, the people of Gonzales were ordered to surrender a Mexican cannon they had been given for protection against the Indians. They responded by waving a flag with the words, "Come and Take It." They took the cannon to a prairie southwest of town where the Mexican force was camped and attacked, sending the Mexican troops fleeing to San Antonio, about sixty-five miles to the west.

Four months later, when William Barret Travis called for help in defending the Alamo, thirty-two Texans gathered at Gonzales and rode to San Antonio. These volunteers, four of them between the ages of fifteen and nineteen, fought their way into the besieged fortress. Santa Anna made his final assault March 6, killing all the fighters inside.

A few days later, Sam Houston, commander of the Texas army, arrived at Gonzales and began training recruits. When the Mexican army began pursuing him, Houston ordered the town evacuated and burned. He retreated to the Colorado River, then the Brazos, then the San Jacinto. There on April 21, 1836, Houston attacked Santa Anna's camped army, winning a resounding victory.

The year I was born, construction began on a new museum that would memorialize the "Immortal 32" who died at the Alamo. The Gonzales Memorial Museum, one of several historical museums built in Texas during that time, contains the "Come and Take It" cannon.

As a seventh grader, I took a special interest in the heroism of the Gonzales volunteers. My seventh-grade history class presented a play on the Battle of the Alamo to the junior and senior high school student body. I had the honor of playing Colonel Travis. (I did not, however, receive a Hollywood contract for my performance.) I will never forget how I, as Travis, drew that line in the sand with my sword. Our battle cry was "Victory or death."

Before I learned anything about Texas history, Gonzales to me was just "town." It was where my family went on Saturday to buy flour, sugar and other staples. It was where we went to church and visited Grandma and Grandpa Vackar, who lived on St. Vincent Street. It was where I went to school and played football.

During the late 1930s, we lived on the Foster place south of town off Highway 183. In 1940, with the aid of a Farm Security loan, we moved to our home place near the San Marcos River west of town. It was this area, where the San Marcos River flows into the Guadalupe, that attracted the town's founding fathers in the 1820s. The rich, river-bottom land plus the ample rainfall (more than thirty inches a year) brought cotton planters in the 1850s as well as my German ancestors in the 1890s. They were also drawn by the mild winters, abundant fish and wildlife, and wooded areas that provided materials for building homes and wood for domestic fires.

In the 1930s and 1940s, Gonzales was a town of between three and four thousand people. The town was laid out on the east bank of the Guadalupe, on the same plan it had under Mexican rule (the town was rebuilt on the original site after it was burned in the Revolution). In addition to the red brick courthouse (built in 1896) and the post office, the town had a gin, cotton mill, feed store, movie theater, domino hall, several churches and an assortment of cafes, grocery stores and drugstores.

Today, as I look back at Gonzales and my childhood, I can see a connection between the people who lived in Gonzales when I was growing up and those who lived there a century earlier. I believe the citizens of Gonzales who fought in the Revolution created a spirit and a heritage that prepared their descendants to fight the challenges that would come in the early twentieth century.

James Michener, in his book *Texas*, sums up how I feel about the Gonzales volunteers. "In the entire history of Texas there would be none braver that these thirty-two from Gonzales, for each man in this heroic file could say to himself, between thundering heartbeats: I know I'm marching to almost certain death, and I know it's insane, but I prize freedom above life itself."

Adversity may not build character, but it does reveal it.

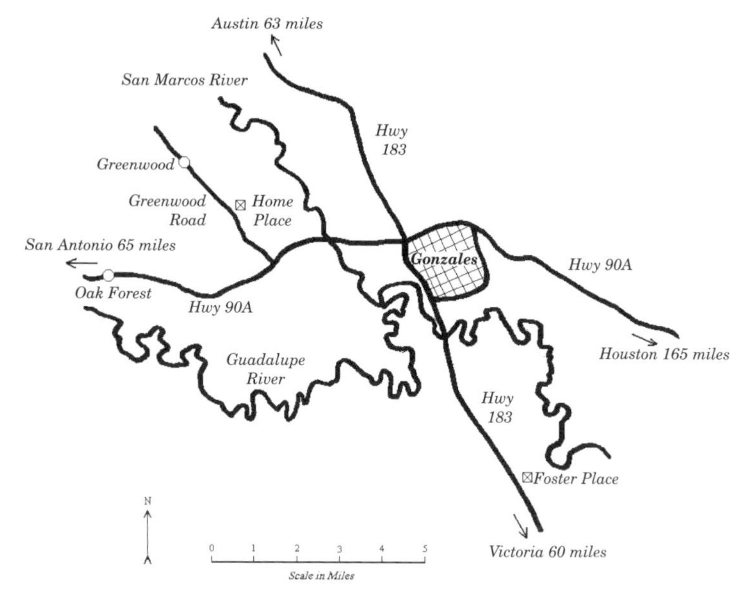

Gonzales Area.

Gonzales County Courthouse.

The Partnership

During the Depression every aspect of life was critical. One of the most critical was having a true marriage partnership. Had Mom and Dad had anything less, life would have been much more difficult.

Mom and Dad met in Gonzales in 1927 when she was eighteen and he was twenty-five. I remember seeing pictures that showed Dad to be quite dapper in his early years. Charlie Schrader always took pride in his appearance. A handsome bachelor with a gentle manner and a kind heart, he caught Mom's attention right away. His black Model T Ford probably also peaked her interest. Mom's beautiful blue eyes and infectious laugh would have been an attraction for any man. But I suspect it was her wit, sharp intellect and vibrant personality that won Dad over.

They married in 1928. That year of courtship gave the two families time to overcome the only major obstacle to their union: Mom was Czech and Dad was German. In the 1920s that was not a totally acceptable combination. In addition, Grandma Vackar was a frail woman who depended on Mom to do much of the cleaning and cooking, and losing her oldest daughter would create quite a void in the house. But Grandpa Vackar must have known that Dad would be a loving husband and a conscientious provider. So when Dad asked for Mom's hand, Grandpa gave a typical Czech response: "The hell you say." Translated, that meant, "I guess it's OK, if it's best for her."

Mom and Dad spent their fifty-seven years together working to improve the lives of their three children and the people in their community. Their tireless energy, mental toughness, positive attitude and sense of humor combined for a winning formula that sustained all of us during difficult times. Long before anyone had heard of women's lib, my father honored and respected my mother's talent and ability. She performed her duties in a bare-bones environment with no conveniences: initially, no electricity and no running water and for many years, no telephone. Dad's duties were equally difficult. A farmer, he dealt with the relentless pressure and anxiety created by the unpredictable weather, the volatile economic market, poor working conditions and in later years, the crippling effects of a drought. But these two soul mates began their life together with the respect and determination that created a loving environment for the entire family.

This time in American history saw the male and female roles clearly defined. Mom managed the house and garden and dealt with the daily trials and tribulations of raising three active children. Everything she did was from scratch. Our clothes were beautifully sewn and always clean and pressed. The food on the table was nutritious and delicious. Her days were filled with hard work and loving direction.

I once asked my dad why I never saw Mom working in the field. "Son, she did field work, but only once," he said. "We hadn't been married long and your mom had come to the field to help me because we couldn't afford to pay a hand. The cornfield was full of Johnsongrass (a pernicious weed that spreads rapidly and is hard to eradicate). We had to dig it up with a hoe and pull the roots out by hand, and we didn't have work gloves. It was backbreaking work under the hot summer sun. After several hours, I saw that your mom's hands were swollen and bleeding. Tears were running down her cheeks. I took her back to the house in the wagon. That was no place for her—and that was the first and last time she worked in the field."

Mom and Dad worked together like true partners, often sacrificing for each other. Mom did not drive a car. When she had a church function or club meeting in town, Dad would leave his work, regardless of what he was doing, and would willingly drive her there. When Mom took in sewing to earn extra money for the family, Dad helped out whenever he could. An extraordinary seamstress, Mom developed quite a successful cottage industry. She sewed for the entire community—everything from frilly Easter frocks to Halloween costumes. Dad took such pride in her ability, even though she didn't bring in a lot of money—in 1944 a lady's dress cost two dollars! Dad told us that Mom's sewing might occasionally interfere with some of her family obligations and if she had a deadline to meet, we were to pick up the slack around the house. Led by his example, we gave her our admiration and respect.

Their partnership continued to thrive, even as we were growing up and moving on. From the mid-1950s until the mid-1980s, Mom and Dad lived on the farm alone, growing older together. When Dad's health began to fail, we worried what might happen to them in an emergency. Then in the winter of 1984, an ice storm stranded them at the farm for three days. It scared us—and them. We knew Dad's heart would never leave the farm, but we urged our folks to move to town. Better access to medical care, we explained, would give them both greater peace of mind. Faced with the decision, Dad responded simply and directly: "We're going to do what's best for Mom." A difficult task, made easy.

When I think of their partnership, I see Mom and Dad holding hands—it was a soft, gentle gesture of love. The Depression transformed that gesture into a fierce and determined grip.

The "partnership"—Charlie and Gladys Schrader, 1928.

Mom and Dad's first home—and Brother's birthplace—in the Oak Forest community.

Tenant Farming

In 1928, as a newly married couple, Mom and Dad began tenant farming near the Oak Forest community. In 1932, they relocated to a farm owned by Mrs. Foster, a widow who lived in Gonzales. At the time they moved, Brother was three years old. Sis and I came along a little later. The Foster place was our home for eight years.

Tenant farmers were independent contractors who owned their own equipment and supplies. It was their responsibility to pay the landlord a percentage of the harvest: 25 percent of the cotton crop and 33 percent of all the other crops. This was a far cry from the meager life of a sharecropper who had no equipment or investment and received only a small percentage of the crop revenue.

The Foster place had approximately a hundred acres of rich, river-bottom farmland and thirty acres of upland. Dad farmed only seventy-five acres of the river bottom—about all he could handle using mule power. At harvest time, he had to have extra help.

The upland acreage was where we had our house and farm buildings. Mrs. Foster, who my parents always referred to as kind and honest, provided not only the house but also the outhouse, the chicken house, the barn, stables and the garage. We also had a garden and a pasture for three or four mother cows and their calves.

The house was larger than most tenant houses—approximately 800 square feet. The exterior was made from one-by-twelve planks of common pine lumber, and one-by-four runners that covered the cracks where the one-by-twelves came together. The wood was gray and showed its age. It's doubtful the house had ever been painted. It was built on a pier-and-beam foundation. The piers were mesquite logs placed deep into the ground, protruding about two and a half feet. This put the house three feet off the ground. The house had a cedar-shake roof that leaked like a sieve. When it rained, every available pot and pan was put into service to catch the rainwater coming through the roof. But a shingle roof was far better than one of tin. Tin carried a connotation of being poor because it was used on outhouses and barns.

The house had three bedrooms, a kitchen with a dining area, and an add-on shed. There were no closets or bathrooms. The house was a "shotgun" design. I think it was called that because one shotgun blast could be fired through the entire house without hitting a wall.

Some of the rooms had no interior walls, just exposed studs. The windows and doors had screens, but judging from the buzzing sounds we heard at night, I don't think all the screens were mosquito-proof. The living room had a linoleum floor that was warm in the winter and, for some reason, cool in the summer. It felt good to take midday naps on the linoleum during those hot months. The kitchen had a wood-burning cookstove, a free-standing cabinet and shelves on the wall. One shelf held a rectangular-shaped, wooden water bucket with a long-handle dipper that served as the water station. An oilcloth covered the table.

A barbed-wire fence kept the cows and their droppings away from the house. The fenced-in yard had little grass in the spring and even less the rest of the year. In the dry, hot summers, dust blew through the open windows and doors, covering every item in the house. The alternative was to close the windows and doors and suffer the unbearable heat. It was a true dilemma.

Life on the Foster place was not easy. The family managed with no electricity, no running water, mule-drawn farm equipment and little money. But we were young, determined and proud. Better times just had to be a part of our future—and eventually they were.

The Foster Place — where Sis and I were born and the Schrader's home from 1932 to 1940.

Health and Home Remedies

The Schrader family always enjoyed good health. We had a few minor ailments and the usual cuts and bruises that came with growing up. For those, there were home remedies. The home was where we were treated—and where we were born.

The three Schrader kids were all born during the Depression. Brother was first and came into the world two weeks after the infamous Black Friday on Wall Street in 1929. (The Crash was not a pivotal event in Gonzales; however, the aftermath certainly was.) Brother was born at home in the presence of a doctor. Grandma Vackar did the honors as an ad hoc midwife. After the event, the doctor conducted a routine examination of the newborn and discovered a birth defect. Brother's pinky toes were twice their normal width and had double toenails! This later helped make him a good swimmer.

I, too, was born at home under the direction of a more experienced Grandma Vackar. Good thing—I arrived before the doctor. According to Mom, the doctor's visit was brief. He scanned my anatomy, certified me OK, complimented Grandma for her good work, and left. Dad settled up with him by giving him eight or ten bushels of corn.

In 1934, two years before I was born, Sis came into the world. As I understand it, she was a twin, but Mom had no idea she was carrying two babies. Sis was born first. She was so tiny, no one (Grandma, Dad and Aunt Julia) thought she would survive. Sis' twin, a perfectly formed girl of normal size, was stillborn. The doctor left Mom and Dad to care for Sis as best they could. She had no official weight because there was no scale to measure it. It was estimated that she weighed two and a half pounds. Dad could hold her in the palm of his hand.

The family got organized to save the baby. It was an unusually cold March 23, so an incubator had to be made if she was to survive. Dad heated bricks in the living room potbelly stove. Grandma put Sis in a shoe box and placed the bricks under and around the box to make a warm environment so she could get on with her life. Sis not only survived, she thrived and grew. Later Mom said the Lord took one away but blessed us with a beautiful, healthy baby. Dad said when he looked at Sis in the shoe box, he knew she would always be the apple of his eye. She was special, and if any member of the family forgot that, Dad would remind them.

I don't remember Mom or Dad ever being sick during those years. Their work was too critical and too compelling for them to be ill. They didn't have an alternative; they were too much in demand. And, furthermore, they didn't have the money to get sick. The Good Lord took care of them so they could take care of us.

Dad did have one problem in his mid-forties. He had a couple of abscessed teeth. The dentist said it was "pulling his entire system down." Who knows, maybe the dentist was right. The prevailing mentality led to the radical conclusion: "Pull 'em all out." Dad's store-bought teeth worked well and were not a distraction, but they were still false teeth. Many people were not so lucky; they were victims of shoddy, unprofessional work that added ten years (or more) to their appearance. Many sets of false teeth were apparently too large, leaving the appearance of a gorilla-type mouth or "buck teeth." The gums on some sets were of various colors: bright orange, burnt orange, dark pink, beige or almost as white as the teeth. Some sets were loose-fitting and, when the person spoke, the teeth would clatter—a real distraction. At bedtime, the procedure was to soak the dentures in a glass of water. Dad had no problem leaving them displayed on the kitchen counter, making them impossible to ignore. It grossed us out. Dad saw nothing wrong; they went into his mouth, so what's the big deal seeing them in a glass of water! Luckily, Mom agreed with us, and Dad found a private place for their nightly storage.

The biggest childhood fear I had was polio. It was an obsession. At one point, during the height of the polio epidemic, I imagined a polio witch would attack and give me the disease. This was the only time in my young life I was afraid of the dark. I never told anyone about the fear because the big kids would have made fun of me. The news on radio station WOAI would give daily accounts of the reported cases in San Antonio. Most people called it "polio"; others called it "infantile paralysis," which made it sound even more dreadful. Promotional literature for fundraising to fight the disease had pictures of little kids with their heads sticking out of iron lungs, which added to the horror.

Mom taught Bible school on Saturdays to the kids at the Gonzales Warm Springs Foundation for Crippled Children. I had to go with her once and after that begged not to go again. It was a traumatic scene: kids with their legs in metal braces with brown straps and big buckles, propped up on crutches, struggling to walk. I thought if I couldn't run and play football, I may as well not live. So I prayed faithfully for an end to this horrible disease. In 1954, my prayers were answered. Dr. Jonas Salk, after years of research, developed a vaccine. It was one of the most important days of my life. My dream that this dreaded disease would be conquered had become a reality.

There were few serious health problems in Gonzales. As with most kids, we passed around mumps, measles and chickenpox. Medical science had already given us protection against smallpox, diphtheria, tetanus and whooping cough. Many health problems were brought about by poor hygiene. Poor hygiene did not cause ringworm and impetigo but provided a perfect breeding ground for them. Ringworm was usually on the scalp. It was treated by shaving the area around the reddened ring, making it even more gross in appearance. Then it was coated with Mercurochrome (we called it "monkey blood"), which contained a red dye, drawing further attention to the nasty problem. I asked why the victim didn't wear a cap to cover up the condition. Mom said it had to have air to heal. Impetigo was worse in appearance than ringworm because it often appeared as sores on the face and lips. School officials had to tell kids not to come back to school until their problem cleared up. It was a tough call.

As an active youngster, I had my share of scrapes and cuts from time to time. I still have the scars to prove it. Once I fell and busted my chin climbing a cottonwood tree. Stitches would have avoided a small scar. (Now I have to go slow when I shave.) At age four, I fell against the living room potbelly stove and burned my knee. Treatment: hog lard. Dad put chicken wire around the stove so that wouldn't happen again. I ran into a barbed-wire fence once playing hide-and-seek at night and cut my leg. Treatment: kerosene. I cut my knee with a butcher knife while making a stock for my slingshot. Treatment: kerosene. I stepped on a nail. Treatment: kerosene. I asked Dad why kerosene was such a good cure for so many things. His answer: "It has oil in it."

When I was twelve, I had a problem with seed warts. Four or five cropped up on the back of my hand. A popular explanation for developing warts was that the victim played with frogs. Could have been, because from time to time I did enjoy chasing them down as they tried to escape. I experimented with a couple of home remedies: briskly rub a raw potato on the warts for three consecutive days, or put salt pork directly on the uglies overnight. Neither worked. This was a serious problem for a twelve-year-old who was beginning to discover girls. Motivated by desperation, I burned them off with battery acid. I was ahead of the times because a few years later a product called Ozone Wart Killer hit the market. The principal ingredient was acid, but probably not battery acid.

According to one theory, you can't feel pain in more than one place at a time. If you have a hurt knee and develop a more painful back injury, the pain in your knee diminishes. In those days, this theory was often applied. From it came the principle of counterirritation. Good examples are the skin irritations that develop after applying kerosene, turpentine and other chemicals. Often the cure was worse than the disease. In one procedure, croton oil (a brownish yellow oil that irritated the skin) was applied to the affected area. Then the area was covered with a cloth laced with small needles. Ouch, what a cure!

The following are some of the more interesting ingredients in home remedies:

- Turpentine—a versatile, oil-based product effective for various treatments and also a good paint thinner.
- Kerosene—cheap, easily accessible, an item every household had on hand for night light, starting fires and fuel for cooking and heating.
- Whiskey—a good excuse to have a bottle in the house at all times, and a way to enjoy bad health! Note: white

whiskey was frequently specified because some church denominations felt dark whiskey had a sinful connotation; white whiskey was more "medicinal."

- Honey—a tasty treat when you were ill. Someone in the community always had beehives, so everyone had a ready supply. Often the product lost its taste benefit when mixed with vinegar, salt, kerosene or turpentine.
- Plants, roots, bark and leaves—accessible and free. Whatever strain or species that grew in the area was the best.
- Ashes—always an ample supply. Very safe. No fear of infection since it was sanitized by the heat.

Most remedies were cheap, homegrown and plentiful. Vinegar, salt, salt pork, ashes, soot, lard, pork fat, chewing tobacco and kerosene all fit that criteria.

One indispensable product in our home was Vicks VapoRub. We probably wouldn't have survived a chest cold without this miracle drug. The treatment was a liberal amount of Vicks smeared on a rag and heated from the steam produced by a teakettle. The hot, Vicks-saturated rag was tied around your neck and also applied to your chest overnight. You woke up the next morning feeling much better, with the rag still wrapped around your neck and the bedsheets greasy from the oil-based Vicks. (The skin irritation was part of the price you paid for the cure.)

We had two jars of Vicks (thank goodness) for two different purposes. One jar was used exclusively for the nostrils. This opened up the breathing passages. The other jar was for everything except the nose. Putting a dab down your throat worked for a sore throat. We were careful not to get the jars mixed-up, and I hope we never did (not that it matters now). Another treatment was melting a half teaspoon of Vicks over the teakettle steam and inhaling the vapors, being careful not to inhale too much, or you would irritate the lining inside your nose. Vicks was strong stuff. You could feel it all the way down to the lower quadrant of your lungs. After we got a butane range, Sis and I would melt Vicks over a burner flame. Mom would get mad if we allowed it to catch on fire, but we were just trying to have some fun. In addition to treating respiratory ailments, Vicks was applied on minor cuts and abrasions. It smelled like it was working. Kerosene was also used for cuts and nail penetrations, but I never got the idea it was helping. Kerosene didn't smell like medicine; Vicks did. Sixty years later, Vicks VapoRub is still on the drugstore shelves, and the product line has greatly expanded.

Except when I was going to school or church, I didn't wear shoes. I even played football through elementary school barefoot. My bare feet picked up quite a few thorns, especially when I ventured into the woods. Mom usually could pick them out with a sewing needle, but occasionally a big mesquite thorn needed the salt-pork treatment. Mom placed the bacon on my foot, wrapped a rag around it and secured it with a safety pin. The next morning, like magic, the thorn was on the salt pork and out of my foot.

We always had a calendar from Spooner's Drugstore hanging on the wall in the kitchen. It never seemed to change its advertisement. Years later I learned the reason: businesses pushed high-profit items. One product always on the calendar was Cardui (pronounced CAR doo eye). This miracle drug was taken to relieve a woman's monthly discomfort, anxiety and general blahs. An old-time pharmacist friend said he bought it in large quantities and sold it at a handsome profit. My guess is that the contents were 95 percent alcohol and 5 percent color and flavoring. The man of the house encouraged his wife to take a generous dose at frequent intervals, even before the symptoms occurred. The ol' boy's hope was that the medicine would put the lady in a responsive mood.

Another item advertised on the calendar was Black Draught. Back in those days, constipation was a frequent problem, or at least a perceived problem. It was important that everyone, young and old, be "cleaned out" on a regular basis. Why nature needed constant assistance, I'll never know. Almost every home had a hot-water bottle with an enema tube hanging on the back of the bathroom door. Thank goodness Mom thought nature was doing a good job for me. Occasionally, though, I did have the Black Draught treatment. It was horrible tasting, and it tasted even worse when you knew you didn't need it.

The old adage, "Necessity is the mother of invention" applied to many home remedies. Some worked, some failed, but they all got an "A" for effort. Here's a list:

Arthritis:

- Place a magnet directly on the affected area. (Comment: magnet therapy has become a popular treatment within the past ten years.)

Athlete's foot:

- Step in fresh cow dung.

Bleeding:

- Apply kerosene, but not too much because it will make you blister.
- Make a paste from chimney or stove soot and hog lard. Smear a liberal amount on and around the area.

Burns:

- Mix table salt and warm water. Saturate a rag with the mixture and apply to the burn. (Comment: a classic example of counterirritant)

- Use lard and flour mixture on the burn. (Comment: very counterproductive—it holds in the heat.)
- Apply axle grease to the burn. (Comment: same as above)

Colds:

- Drink white whiskey and honey. (Comment: omit the honey.)
- Eat onions roasted in ashes. (Comment: counterirritant)
- Drink a mixture of honey and vinegar. (Comment: it's hard to find two items more incompatible.)
- Boil pine needles and make a strong tea. (Comment: did not specify dry or green needles)

Colic:

- Feed the baby breast milk with one drop of kerosene. (No comment)

Croup:

- Squeeze the juice out of a roasted onion and drink.
- Drink a mixture of onion juice and honey.
- Mix lard, turpentine and kerosene. Spread the mixture inside a wool cloth, place it over the chest and around the neck, and keep it on all night. (Comment: turpentine and kerosene mixed together create a major counterirritant.)
- Put a drop of turpentine in a spoonful of sugar and eat. (No comment)

Diarrhea:

- Drink tea made from red oak bark.

Earache:

- Put several drops of sewing-machine oil in the ear. (Comment: one person claimed it worked because the body is a machine, too.)

- Warm a spoonful of urine and put a few drops in the ear. (No comment)

Gallbladder trouble:

- Take a teaspoon of pure corn whiskey and Black Draught.

Headache:

- Smear brow with crushed onions.

Hiccups:

- Take a spoonful of peanut butter.

Sores:

- Put butter around the sore so a dog will lick it. The dog's saliva will cure it.

Some home remedies were over the edge. And there were some remedies for which there was no known disease. One such remedy was drinking pure corn whiskey straight out of the bottle. This was before alcoholism was considered a disease.

Home remedies, like other aspects of Depression living, were created because folks had to solve a problem or fulfill a need. Some remedies worked, and some did not. Some were counterproductive, and some were downright dangerous. Some were a success because they coincided with the problem running its course. But any home remedy was better than nothing because it gave hope. I once asked Dad how some of these home remedies came about. Were they really used, and were they successful? His answer: "If you ever had a child cry all night with pain, you were ready to try anything, regardless of how far-fetched it seemed."

Most medicine was practiced in the home, not in the hospital. Most people thought that if you were admitted to the hospital, you should take your Bible with you. Chances were good you might never leave alive.

Our family doctor was a hero, working in the trenches against the perils of the Depression. Like many doctors, he did a lot of charity work. The measure of his success was not money, but rather healing the sick.

One family doctor in Gonzales loved kids and had a passion for football. He was the football team doctor and traveled with us to out-of-town games. He loved to tell stories, hoping to share his blessings with young people by impressing upon them that the greatest rewards in life come from serving others. He also happened to be the most compassionate person I have ever known. He was to Gonzales what Mother Theresa was to India.

Health insurance was almost nonexistent. When people got sick or injured, they seemed to find a way to pay the medical expenses. Dad gave our doctor two shoats (young pigs) for setting Brother's broken arm. Another time Dad was awakened in the middle of the night by a neighbor who had a sick child who needed a doctor immediately. The neighbor said ten dollars would help if Dad had it. Dad gave him twenty, which was all he had. "Pay me when you can." It didn't take long for the loan to be repaid.

Fortunately, the Schrader family rarely had to call the doctor or resort to home remedies. I attribute our good health to nutritious food and good food-handling practices. We all worked hard, which provided us with sufficient exercise, and we practiced good hygiene. (Lye soap worked great as a sanitizer.) Most important, we picked good parents.

A New Era

The turning point in our lives came in 1940 when we were awarded a loan from the Farm Security Administration. This was one of FDR's New Deal programs established in 1937. It changed the lives of many farm families.

The program was administered by the county judge who selected a committee of respected people from the community to award the loans. The criteria were similar to those for a standard bank loan. The program was successful because it benefited those who wanted a chance and were willing to work. The participants were monitored by the local committee. Dad dealt with friends as opposed to government bureaucrats. Mom diligently kept the required records of all financial activities throughout the year. In the fall of every year, the committee hosted a potluck picnic at one of the farms for all the recipients, the committee members and the county judge. In the fall of 1941, we had the picnic at our farm. Mom and Dad were beaming with pride. It had been a wonderful two years.

The breakdown of our farm loan was as follows: 130 acres at $35 per acre equals $4,550. Improvements, which included the house, garage, outhouse, water supply (windmill and cistern) and an orchard, came to $1,400. So the total principal was $5,950 ($4,550 plus $1,400). The payout was $180 per year for 40 years (that equals $7,200, so the interest was $1,150). Dad turned down 90 acres at

$11 per acre that would have extended our property to the San Marcos River. He felt another $990 on the loan was too much of an obligation, and he was comfortable with 130 acres, the size of the Foster place.

We called the new farm “the home place.” It was five miles west of Gonzales in the Greenwood community. The farm consisted of a hundred acres of land close to the San Marcos River. Thousands of floods over millions of years had made the soil fertile. There was one downside: the land was infested with that insidious devil, Johnsongrass. But that was a mere bump in the road. That problem would be solved with hard work.

The upland consisted of thirty acres, perfect for our needs. Where the valley ended, a small hill ascended for about 150 yards. At the bottom of the hill was a well with wonderful sweet water. A hundred yards up the hill were two beautiful, large live oak trees waiting to be part of our backyard. The front of the house would look down on the beautiful river valley, so we could sit on the porch and watch our crops grow. The balance of the thirty acres would be pasture for our cows. In the spring and early summer, an abundance of native grass would provide excellent grazing for our cattle, which consisted of five mother cows and their calves. There was also additional grazing land in the valley that was not under cultivation. The upland had a large supply of mesquite trees we could use for fence posts and firewood.

The design of a Farm Security home was simple and straightforward. There were different elevations, so no two looked exactly alike. While our home was being built, we would finish our Saturday shopping and socializing and motor out to the construction site to check the progress. The next day, after church, we would take another trip, and slowly walk the grounds, inspecting the frame and foundation. Dad and Mom would discuss plans for the rest of the compound. I marveled at those live oak trees in the backyard, visualizing the perfect place for my treehouse. Sis picked out the right spot for her swing.

One visit stands out in my memory. Just before we topped the hill, before we could see the construction site, Dad stopped the car and suggested we walk the rest of the way. Dad had been out to examine the site the day before. We all wondered what was up. As we walked over the hill, we jumped for joy. The exterior of the house was covered with white paint. I looked at the tears rolling down Mom's cheeks. Dad was so proud. We would soon realize the American dream of home ownership.

Our floor plan was a stroke of genius. How could so much be put into a 1,000-square-foot house? The kitchen/dining area and living room comprised the front of the house, and the only area that was heated (by wood stoves). In the back of the house were three bedrooms, with closets, a hall and a bathroom. We never thought the house was too small for a family of five. Some of the rooms had wallpaper; others were painted white. The floors were pine. We had running water with two faucets, one in the kitchen and the other in the bathroom. There was a foot tub (a mini washtub about a third the size of a No. 3 washtub) that served as the sink in the bathroom. It would do until times got better. A claw-foot bathtub would come later. For now we would bathe in a No. 3 washtub.

Mom was excited about her new kitchen. She had a shiny, black, wood-burning stove and a large counter for food preparation. She didn't have to go to the well for water, and she had plenty of room to incorporate an icebox. This was a new era in her life.

The house had a pier-and-beam foundation, which elevated it about thirty inches above the ground. The north wind whipped under the house, creating arctic temperatures in the winter. The house came with no insulation. My bedroom was on the north side, and Brother and I shared a bed. He told me that it was only fair to let me sleep by the window at least half the time. This really made me happy until I realized I slept next to the window in the winter and he slept next to the window in the summer. Just another reminder that Brother was older. Later on, when his social activities increased, he would come home long after I was in bed. On cold nights he would simply move me over and take my warm spot. I hated that. It once got so cold in our bedroom that the liquid Shinola Shoe Polish and the Vaseline Hair Tonic froze in our closet. Mom layered the covers on our bed, and this kept us warm. She alternated homemade quilts with newspapers. I don't remember the number of layers that were necessary on a cold night, but it worked.

On cold mornings, Dad was always up at least an hour before Mom, building a fire in the cookstove and living room stove so we had a warm house when we woke. It never occurred to me then, but matches were a great invention. The back area of the house was not heated and was closed off by a hallway door. Summer nights were fairly comfortable. The house was situated on a hill, so the southerly breezes cooled us as we slept.

Our farm was not just a house and land for crops; it was a food-supply center that produced 95 percent of the food we consumed. We needed buildings for cows, pigs and chickens. The lumber came from an old farmhouse and a barn that were already on the property. Dad and Uncle Walter designed and built the structures, with the aid of an occasional helper. Uncle Walter was a good carpenter (he later took up the trade full-time). They did a good job because these buildings are still standing (some barely) today. Overall the building project required more than two years to complete. Dad and Uncle Walter had to keep their day jobs during this period, so it was a part-time endeavor.

The barn had stables for the milk cows, separate stables for the mules, and racks, hooks and shelves for equipment. Fences were built in front of the barn as a holding area for calves (to assure the return of the mother cows after a day of grazing in the pasture) . In back of the barn was a large pigpen and shed. In the backyard of the house was a combination smokehouse and wash shed. Some distance from the house, between the barn and the outhouse, was a chicken house. The reason for the remote location: chickens eat a lot and excrete a lot.

Although the farm perimeter and property-line fences were established and in pretty good condition, the cross fences and other interior fences had to be constructed. As was the case with most things on the farm, fence building required old-fashioned hard work. The holes had to be dug with a manually operated posthole digger. Soil variance made this job difficult, especially when there was too much caliche or gravel. The fence posts were cut from mesquite trees. Mesquite wood is one of the hardest woods, which made for difficult chopping. The upside was that the posts were incredibly strong; some are still in the ground holding up barbed wire after sixty years.

This wonderful country home was the perfect place to grow up. I was four when we moved there, and this farm would be my home for the next fourteen years. I can't think of anything that I would change. The move from the Foster place to the home place was a pivotal time in our lives. Seeing pictures in *Life* magazine of hungry families waiting in line outside soup kitchens for a meal only reinforced our feelings of good fortune. We knew we were truly blessed. We had our health and if we worked hard, we would continue to prosper.

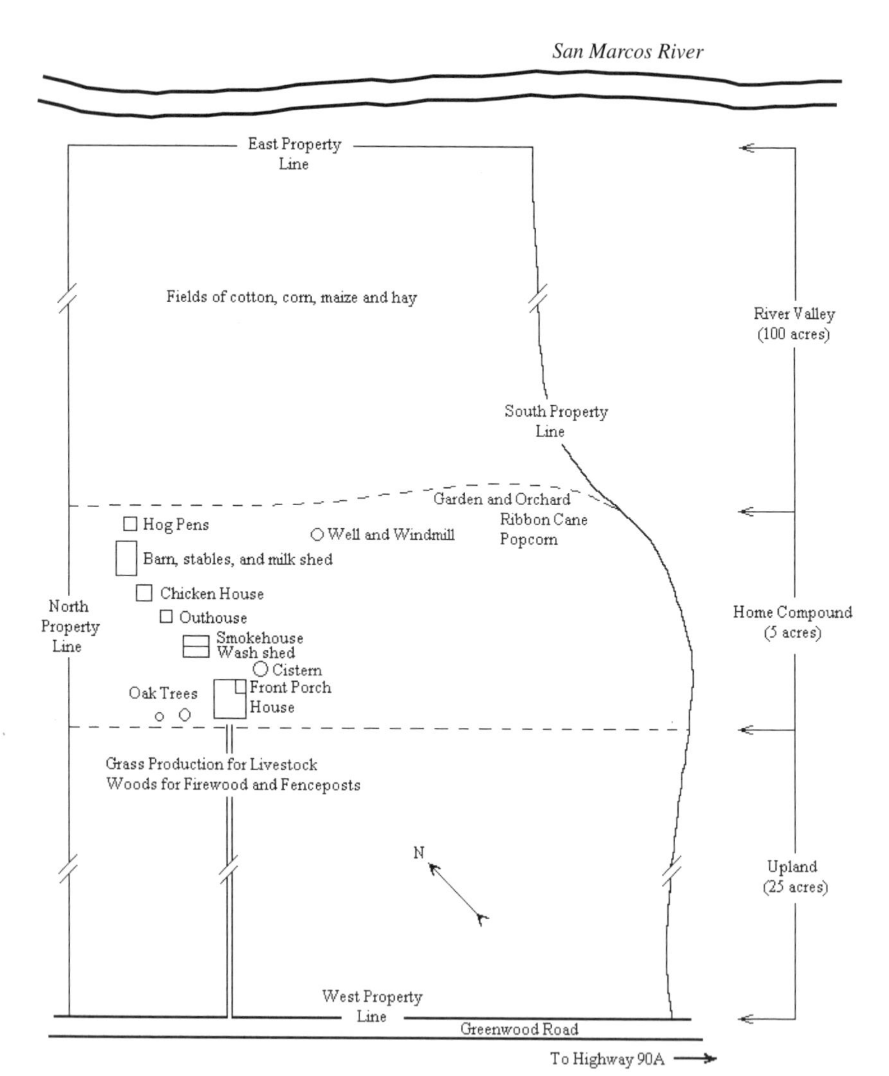

The Home Place.

Front view of the Home Place.

Buddy, Sis and Brother—
first year at the Home Place.

The barn — site of the Annual Rat Killing.

Home place — backyard with its wonderful oak tree— perfect for swings and tree houses.

The outhouse. A well-thought-out design.

Water: A Precious Commodity

In 1943 I attended a funeral for the first time. Mom said that I, as a seven-year-old, was quite bewildered about the whole process. Among my many questions was: "Who is this man and what happened to him?" She told me he was a well digger and he had once helped a friend of Dad's put in his well. The funeral helped me appreciate the difficulty involved in finding a precious commodity: water.

Well digging was a dangerous occupation. The standard well hole was four to six feet in diameter. When the hole got too deep to toss the dirt out by shovel, the well digger bailed out the dirt with a bucket and pulley, one bucket at a time. As he dug, he lined the walls of the well with bricks and mortar, logs, rocks or timber. Sometimes, if the soil texture was strong enough, he supported the walls after the water was found. Either way, the deeper the hole became, the greater the possibility of a cave-in. Giving up on a location and starting the process at another site was a judgment call. It was discouraging to dig a fifty-foot hole, pronounce it a failure, and start over again. This was a job for only the stouthearted.

If you were lucky, you found water at thirty feet. But sometimes the digging might continue for sixty, eighty or even a hundred feet. The digger had to descend into the hole by means of pulleys. It was a long and laborious task inside a deep hole, with only a lantern, a shovel and a bucket.

When you hit water, it was a joyous day—especially if the water tasted clean and sweet. Anticipating the taste was exciting. Good-tasting water was a blessing and a tremendous asset to your property. Some water, however, had sulfur in it. Sulfur made it smell like rotten eggs. It was OK for consumption, but the odor made it undesirable for drinking—and that was a tragedy.

A qualified well digger could often tell by the topography of the land where water would be found. Some farmers used the ancient "divining rod" method. The diviner lightly held a rod, usually a willow branch, as he walked about. The rod would bend down, supposedly of its own volition, above the water source. Many landowners had great faith in this method, and I understand it is still often used today.

On the Foster place, we shared a well with Uncle Walter and Aunt Julia. Hand pumps were available to draw the water, but we couldn't afford one, so we used buckets and a pulley. For efficiency, there was a bucket on each end of a rope. The gardens were located near the well for irrigation, and that was limited to small plants. The one-bucket-at-a-time process prevented large-scale irrigation.

The water was drawn and poured into a fifty-five-gallon drum. Uncle Walter's drum was on a skid and was transported to the house by mule. Dad had rigged up a cart from an old wagon. It consisted of two wheels, a platform for the barrel and a singletree that hooked the cart to our mule. The rig resembled a cannon, so that's what we called it.

We had a cistern at the house that caught rainwater from the roof, but the container leaked so badly it never held much water. There were too many holes in the cistern and not enough rain. The leaks forced us to deploy the "cannon" shortly after a rain. We parked the "cannon" by the back door, near the kitchen, for easy access. We kept it covered to minimize the invasion of bugs and varmints. Although the leaky container did not contribute much to our water supply, it did provide a muddy playground for the neighborhood kids. Sis and Cousin Joyce practiced their domestic skills making mud pies.

In the house, we had a bucket and dipper for drinking water. Another bucket provided water for all other domestic needs.

We took daily sponge baths using two cloths: one with soap and water, another with plain water for rinsing. Once-a-week tub baths were common. Water was heated on the kitchen stove and transported to a No. 3 washtub in the add-on room. The tub was hardly large enough for an adult, so my guess is that Mom and Dad knelt or stood in the tub while they washed and rinsed, splashing the water on their bodies. There was a definite pecking order for fresh, hot water. I was the youngest of the five, so, naturally, I was last. By then, the water was chilly, and the soap residue made bathing even more undesirable. But I had no choice. Once a week, and I certainly needed it, I took a bath.

The move in 1940 to the home place was a giant step forward. No more drawing water, no more hauling water with the "cannon." We had running water in the house! Even though it was only two faucets (in the kitchen and bathroom), it was a wonderful advancement.

When friends and relatives came to see our new home and admire our beautiful farm, one of the main interests was our well. Dad would draw the bucket up and use the dipper to scoop out the cool, clear liquid. Each taster would close his eyes, smack his lips and concentrate on the flavor of the water as the dipper was passed around. The taste was a little sweet and a perfect temperature for drinking. Dad was proud of his well. He knew water was the lifeblood of his farm.

To have running water in the house and the wash shed, we had to pump the water with a windmill and hold it in the cistern that we bought as part of our Farm Security loan. The windmill was placed directly over the well. Wind would blow against the wheel blades at the top, and gears would move a plunger rod up and down, bringing the water to the surface. The plunger assembly had a valve that would keep the water from going back down and instead be diverted into the cistern.

The weight of the water in the cistern would force the water through the pipe when a faucet in the house was opened. On rare occasions, the water level became too low for this to function. The water would fall below that level because we didn't have enough wind to turn the windmill. When this happened, we were back to drawing the water by bucket.

The wellhead was covered by a stone-and-mortar circular structure that stood three feet above the ground. The top layer was concrete, approximately four inches thick. In the center was the plunger and next to it was an opening, eighteen inches square, for bucket access. Immediately over the access hole was a pulley for lowering and raising the bucket. The lid over the opening was thick and heavy, with a wide metal strap for a handle. The reason for such a heavy lid was to make it impossible for small children to lift the lid and fall in.

Even with running water, Mom would send me to our closest neighbor about a quarter mile away for a bucket of rainwater they caught from the roof in their cistern. That was nature's water—soft and free of minerals. Mom used it exclusively for washing her and Sis' hair. Mom said the water made their hair shine.

Life was getting better. We had running water in the bathroom, but for the first couple of years we still used a No. 3 washtub for bathing. In 1942 we got a bathtub—a beautiful white porcelain tub with claw feet. Taking a bath was not so bad anymore. I could even have my own fresh water. But we were still heating bath water on a wood stove (we had no thought of anything comparable to a hot-water heater), so there was a limit to the hot water supply. I never understood why it was so important to take these baths—I much preferred to rinse off in the creek or tie a hose to a tree in the backyard and play in the spray.

Wash Day

It's funny how childhood memories can bring back sights and smells from long ago that remain as alive and vivid as they were back then. One such memory is the fragrant smell of Mom's freshly laundered towels, and the feeling of crawling into bed between two of her soft, clean cotton sheets. Maybe it was the sunshine or maybe it was the gentle breezes that tossed everything about on the clothesline, but I will never forget wash day. It gave each week a clean start and reminded me how dedicated my mother was to the well-being of her family.

Washing clothes was perhaps the most physically challenging of any job for the housewife at that time. Mom endured this laborious task every week until after World War II when electric washing machines became available. In the summer when school was out, Sis helped with laundry, but most of the year Mom did it alone. Clothes got dirty every day, and clothes were washed every week. The customary wash day was Monday, weather permitting, but without fail, wash day happened every week.

Brother, Sis and I had been trained to be conservative with our clothes to minimize the amount of our dirty laundry. This was another way Dad protected Mom from undue work caused by thoughtless kids. It was our responsibility to care for our clothes, hang them up or fold them for re-wear when possible. There were five towel racks in the bathroom; one for every member of the family and an allotment of two towels per-person per-week. When I was younger, one was plenty for me.

In the backyard, approximately fifteen yards from the back door, was a barn-type structure that served as both a wash shed and a smokehouse. The smokehouse, which was in the back, was used for processing, curing and storing meat. The wash shed portion faced the house. A wall on the north side protected Mom from the cold winter winds, and a wall on the east side shielded her from the midday sun. The south side was open.

On the walls of the wash shed hung four galvanized No. 3 washtubs. I assume Dad made the wash benches. They appeared to be custom-made to fit Mom's height. Washing required repetitive bending, twisting, stooping and lifting. Mom had been performing this task since she was a child, so she was in excellent condition to handle it. She never complained of back problems, but I'm sure the physical demands of the job occasionally took their toll. But, as usual, Mom never complained about anything.

The sixteen-gallon wash pot was located a few feet from the business center of the wash shed, close to the tubs on the bench but far enough from the work area to avoid the smoke and heat of the fire. The large, heavy, cast-iron pot was designed to withstand enormous heat and was durable enough to be passed down to future generations. The outside was coated with layers of black soot and grime. The inside was smooth and shiny, thanks to the boiling lye-soap water. The rounded, contoured bottom made it easier to remove the hot water with buckets. Three stubby legs rested on bricks that elevated the pot six inches above the ground. This maximized the air flow and kept the fire burning. The fire was built around and under the pot.

Before I inherited the job, Brother was responsible for arranging the firewood. He had to have the wood ready so the water would be boiling hot by the time Mom was ready to start washing. If Brother failed to stack the wood on Sunday afternoon, Dad made him get up early Monday morning before school to do the job. I got involved prematurely because I wanted to be part of the fire-building process. Brother was thrilled. After a short time, my fascination with fire-building diminished, but there was no way I could give the job back to Brother. I was stuck with it.

One giant step forward on wash day was being able to turn on the water faucet in the wash shed instead of carrying it bucket by bucket from the "cannon." That became possible when we moved from the Foster place to the home place. After the wash pot was filled with water, Dad doused the firewood with kerosene and waited a couple of minutes to allow it to soak into the wood before starting the fire. By the time we left for school, the water was ready.

Mom transferred the hot water by bucket from the wash pot to the first two tubs in line on the bench. The first tub, which contained lye-soap shavings, had a scrub board with two legs that stood above the warm, soapy water. The cleaning concept was basic: after the clothes were saturated with soapy water, they were rubbed against the corrugated metal board until the spots or soil were dissolved.

Lye soap was used for cleaning everything except the human body. (Mom would jokingly threaten to wash my hair with lye soap if I didn't do an acceptable job.) Lye soap was used for clothes, dishes, floors and all other cleaning needs. Lye was extremely dangerous, a fact emphasized on the can. It depicted a horned devil with a long, barbed tail, pitchfork in hand and red flames erupting from its mouth and the top of its head. It was completely surrounded by fire. A clear point to the consumer that the product was lethal. As I remember it, the brand name was Red Devil Lye.

Mom made two piles of clothes on the ground near the wash pot. The pile that required only light washing went directly into the washtub with the scrub board. She scrubbed these items and agitated them by hand in the wash water. She squeezed or lightly wrung the items and placed them in rinse tub No. 1. She agitated them by hand again and placed them in rinse tub No. 2, the final rinse. This tub contained cool water and a small amount of bluing. This was a blue liquid that came in a blue bottle and gave a blue sparkle to the rinse water. It was widely used to make white clothes whiter—at least that was the prevailing belief.

The second pile was for heavily soiled clothes. Mom put those in the wash pot, added lye-soap shavings, and let them boil. She removed the hot clothes from the water with a sawed-off broom handle and stacked them on a bench to cool and drain. After frequent use, the lye water would eat into the wood handle, giving it a soft, fuzzy texture. Once the clothes had cooled, Mom put them in the washtub and followed the scrub-rinse-rinse cycle described earlier.

After completing the final rinse, Mom wrung out the clothes and tossed them into a fourth tub on the floor at the end of the bench. It was an old tub that leaked, but it was adequate for damp items headed for the clothesline.

Some clothes, including Dad's work clothes, sheets and jeans, required more twisting and wringing than Mom could manage, so Dad helped wring out the items before he returned to the field for his afternoon shift. Later in their marriage, Dad bought Mom a hand-operated wringer that attached to the final rinse tub. It made the job easier but not necessarily faster.

Once the clothes were wrung out, Mom would drag the tub to the clothesline by inserting a towel through the handle. This method kept her from lifting the heavy tub. Mom, in her flowery sunbonnet with the clothespin bag hung over her shoulder, would go to the side yard to hang the clothes on the line. I loved that image of her.

For some shirts and pants to look their Sunday best, they had to be starched. Mom dissolved a couple of tablespoons of Faultless Starch, a powdered compound, in a dishpan of hot water. She dipped the clothes into the solution and hung them out to dry. The next day, before ironing the clothes, she sprinkled them with water and rolled them up individually so they would be damp and easier to iron.

Until 1943, ironing methods were still centuries old. The process required two irons, each made of cast iron and each weighing approximately five pounds. The irons were heated on the wood stove. Lifting a heavy, red-hot iron from the stove and maneuvering it around on collars and sleeves was no job for weaklings. She started with one iron, which stayed hot for about ten minutes of pressing, returned it to the stove and then used the other. It took Mom about four hours to iron the family's clothes. When the outside temperature was ninety degrees or more, the heat in the kitchen on ironing day must have been unbearable. But Mom would not allow any of us to leave the house with wrinkled clothes, especially when we went to church or social events.

In 1942, when I was six, Mom began her sewing business. She was unable to devote most of Tuesday to ironing, so she hired Rosie Lampkin. She was nicknamed "Rosie Red" because she always wore something red. Rosie worked for other families in the area on other days of the week. Had there been a poverty line, she (like many other blacks) would have been well below it. By doing the ironing and other cleaning, Rosie took a tremendous burden from Mom and quickly became part of the family. We looked forward to her coming every week. She would tell Dad, Brother and me how good we looked in our neatly pressed shirts and trousers. Though her life was hard, she made life a pleasure for herself and people around her. She was an unforgettable individual we all greatly respected and admired.

After our house was wired for electricity, Mom got an electric iron. She couldn't get an electric washing machine until after the war, and by then, we were old enough to be responsible for the care of our own clothes. For Mom, wash day had become easier. Life was good.

Recipe for Homemade Lye Soap

Lye soap is an excellent stain remover. It's the standard for dishes, floors and clothes (but avoid using on delicate garments).

24 lbs. lard

4 gallons water

4 12-oz. cans of lye

Suspend a large cast-iron kettle over an open fire. Add water and lard; stir with a big wooden paddle. Slowly add the lye to the water. Never add water to lye – the results can be explosive. Continue stirring as the mixture boils to avoid foaming and overflow.

When waxy strings form as you lift the paddle, the mixture is done (about 45-90 minutes). Remove from heat, and sprinkle with cold water to settle the foam. Allow to cool, then cut into wedges. The soap will last longer if you wait until the wedges are hard and dry before using.

Makes about 35 pounds of soap

(Good luck!)

The wash shed, smokehouse and sleeping quarters for Butch and Pudge.

Electricity: The Miracle of Light

The first and only time my second-grade teacher, Mrs. Morman, kissed me was the day I told her we had electricity. To me, it was truly a miracle. Most people have no concept of life without electricity. I was born into that world and to this day I am obsessive about not wasting it.

Until 1943 our indoor lighting came from a kerosene lamp. The design and capability of this lamp has not changed for hundreds of years. To read and perform close work, you had to be near the lamp, which produced heat as well as light. This was particularly unpleasant on a hot summer night. We would also use the light of the lamp to escort our guests to and from their cars.

Mom and Dad had an emergency plan in the event someone dropped a burning lamp. (Kids were forbidden to carry a lit lamp.) They kept a couple of old cotton-picking sacks under their bed that could be used to smother the fire. Fortunately, we never had an accident. We all developed a skill for functioning without light. Dad was efficient at milking cows in the dark. Our house was small and the furnishings sparse, so we could easily negotiate in the dark.

We once upgraded to a Coleman gas lantern that gave off a bright, white light. Air was pumped into the gas tank, producing a vapor. A lit match would make the vapor burst into flame. This wonderful instrument brightened up the entire room and made reading and homework easier. Now Mom could do needlework without squinting. One night, however, I looked up and screamed—the lantern was on fire! Dad dashed over, picked it up, ran out of the house and threw it in the front yard. It hit the ground and exploded. Dad received a few blisters on his hand, but otherwise he was okay. After that, we went back to the kerosene lamps.

As a kid growing up, I couldn't appreciate how hard it was for my parents to go about their daily activities without electricity. We had no way to cool the house, and our only method of heating was our wood-burning stove. That stove was critical to indoor chores such as washing dishes, ironing, cooking and cleaning, all of which Mom had to do during the day.

A first-grade friend once spent the night with me and was astonished that we had no electricity. My friend joked about it the next day at school—saying that our house was like a coal mine because we used lanterns. I wouldn't have a friend over again until several years later.

Our window to the world was the radio. (The other was the newspaper.) Before electricity, our news and entertainment center was a radio that was large, obtrusive, ugly, unpredictable, inept and a source of many disappointments. Our stations were confined to news and a few entertainment programs, and we were constantly aware of the drain on the batteries. If I remember correctly, the radio was a Philco and used two (maybe three) large batteries, each about twice the size of a shoe box. When the batteries ran out, we often went for long periods before replacing them.

The radio power switch would occasionally malfunction. The radio would frequently and unexpectedly go dead at the most inopportune moments: when we were listening to one of President Roosevelt's fireside chats, while we were waiting for a punch line in *Fibber McGee and Molly*, or when we were guessing the answer to a question posed by Dr. I.Q. in his quiz show. When the radio went dead, we usually solved the problem with a quick flick of the power switch. Like magic, the audio would be restored. For convenience, I would lie on the floor, prop my feet on the side of the radio and flip the switch with my toes.

When the radio wasn't working, the evenings became boring. After homework, there was little to do or say. Rather than sit around in the dim light of the kerosene lamp, we went to bed. We all had ample time for reflection and meditation.

With no electricity, the only timepiece—besides our faithful rooster—we had in the Depression was a wind-up Big Ben clock with bell alarms on the top. During the school year, Dad made a point of keeping it wound because we had to catch the early morning bus. In the summer, when the radio was on the blink, we would go for days not knowing the time of the day (or night). Many appointments were timed to the light of day: "I'll meet you a little after daylight," or "a little before sunset." Dad would rise before daylight (Mom shortly thereafter) and start the work day. When Dad and I were in the field, and it was time for dinner and a mid-day rest, Mom communicated to us by standing in front of the house and waving a white cup towel. I was usually tired and hungry, so Mom didn't have to wave that towel very long before I spotted her. I was ready for a break.

The Rural Electrification Administration was created by FDR in 1936. Its mission was to give all rural America access to electricity. The Roosevelt Administration realized the necessity of providing this valuable resource to the people who fed our country. That need increased after World War II began in 1941 because we needed to raise our own food if we were to win the war. The REA was a co-op, supported by its members and subsidized by the federal government.

In 1942 the REA power line came across our field, made a ninety-degree turn in front of our house and proceeded in a westerly direction. We thought our dream was about to become a reality—we would soon have electric lights! But our excitement was all in vain. We simply did not have the money to buy the necessary wire and sockets for pull-string light bulbs. We endured the agony of having the REA wires attached to our house but not hooked up. The kerosene lamps burned on.

About a year later, we scraped up enough money for the wiring. Uncle Olen, who worked for the telephone company, had enough expertise to wire the house. Even though he was not an electrician, his work has stood the test of time (sixty years). He installed a ceiling light with a pull-string, on/off switch in every room. Uncle Olen surprised us by installing a bulb socket on the front-porch wall. We now had a welcome light, but we were not allowed to turn it on until a guest arrived. This was one of our energy-saving practices; it was part of an ongoing conservation program to make sure we would not exceed our $2.50 minimum monthly bill. The program was a resounding success. I'm sure we never came close to exceeding the minimum kilowatt consumption.

One night when I pulled on the light string in my bedroom, the string broke off inside the socket fixture. The repair had to wait until Uncle Olen could come for a visit. I took the blame, but to this day, I will declare my innocence. I did not pull the string too hard. Everyone was mad at me, especially Brother, because the blackout was in our room. We had disposed of our kerosene lamps, so we had to resort to candles. Uncle Olen came and repaired the light about three weeks later. The outage didn't bother Dad, because it helped keep our bill at the $2.50 minimum.

I remember one evening when the family walked to a neighbor's house for a visit. Returning home, we noticed a light on in our parents' bedroom. We just knew it was foul play. No one could be so negligent as to leave a fifty-watt bulb burning needlessly into the night. Dad picked up a piece of firewood from the wood pile to use as a weapon when he entered the house. Mom and the kids stayed back in fear and anticipation. Of course, no one was there. One of us had simply left a light on. In the future, every time we left the house, there was a walk-through, cross-check and verification.

As time went on, we had wall plugs installed. A plug in the living room allowed us to buy a lamp as well as an electric radio. Because we no longer had the large-battery radio, we had more floor space in the living room. A plug in the kitchen meant Mom could get an electric iron. A plug in our parents' bedroom allowed Mom to get an electric sewing machine, although I still think she could pedal her feet faster than the electric motor could power the machine.

After the war, we got a refrigerator, a small electric fan for the living room and a washing machine. The family treasured these wonderful conveniences because they had been slow in coming. Mom always said, "It's best not to get too much too soon." She endured hardship and deprivation for many years. She had reason to enjoy modern conveniences when they finally arrived.

The last major convenience to arrive was a telephone. Mom and Dad got a phone several years after the kids were grown and gone. During my childhood, important messages were relayed in person, or we used a neighbor's telephone. One Christmas Eve when I was home from college, the sheriff came to our house to deliver season's greetings from the young woman who was my girlfriend at the time. Mom and Dad were in no hurry for a telephone. They had done without one for so many years that they figured they could do without one for a while longer.

Reliable Old Blackie

When Henry Ford's amazing automobile invaded the American scene, it revolutionized society. What an impact it made—especially upon one farm family in Gonzales. I remember the story Dad often told about the first time he saw a car. Someone drove up to his house in 1908 and Dad, having heard of the horseless carriage, ran out to see this new wonder. His little brother reacted differently: he crawled under the bed to escape the monster.

The automobile was a status symbol. Owning one showed the world that you were successful—or at least that you were willing to make sacrifices for the privilege. That is still true today. Car ownership conveys wealth and prestige. It also uniquely defines the occupants.

For much of my childhood, the Schrader automobile told the world we were poor. We owned a 1929 black Model A in bad condition. The production of automobiles, like many other conveniences (refrigerators, tractors and washing machines), halted during World War II. Even if we had had the money, buying a car would have been impossible. We had no choice: we were stuck with Blackie.

Blackie was so ugly that we should have loved her, but somehow we didn't. The right-rear fender had been bent as long as I could remember. Dad never told us how the fender bender happened, but Brother said it was one Saturday night when Mom was directing Dad as he was backing out of the dance-hall parking lot. He backed directly into a large mesquite tree. The fender was ripped away from the body about halfway up. The mishap apparently was the result of a communication breakdown; Mom and Dad each blamed the other.

The fender was never fixed. When we drove faster than thirty miles per hour, the dangling fender would begin to flop. I would stick my head out of the window and yell to Dad to go faster. The increased air current would cause the fender to bang against the bumper, making a clanging noise. Dad, a good sport, obliged and we would both laugh. It wasn't funny to Mom, however. She would say, "Slow down, Charlie. Stop acting so silly."

When we were caught in a rain shower, the windshield wipers didn't work. Brother said the wipers worked off a vacuum. I never knew what that meant, but I did know they did not vacuum. Henry Ford, the genius that he was, anticipated occasional malfunctions and provided a back-up. The passenger could operate the wipers manually from inside the car. This allowed the driver to devote full attention to the road. There was also a hand-operated wiper on the passenger side, but trying to operate both of them at the same time required great dexterity. Mom didn't need to know where we were going as long as Dad did.

I don't think Blackie ever had a gas gauge; if she did, it never worked. The gas tank was between the engine and the fire wall, below and in front of the windshield. Sounds dangerous, but I never heard of a Model A catching on fire or exploding due to the location of the gas tank. We measured the gas level by removing the gas cap and inserting a sawed-off broomstick into the tank. Marks on the broomstick indicated the amount of gas we had left. This measuring device was stored under the driver's seat.

The upholstery material was an off-white, heavy-duty duck; the same material used for cotton-picking sacks. Years of wear and tear took its toll on Blackie's interior.

After several years, Mom made a new set of seat covers using the same fabric. She bought the material at the Gonzales Cotton Mill, where it was manufactured. She was a highly skilled seamstress, so the seat covers fit perfectly without a single wrinkle.

We drove Blackie on three different roads on the five-mile stretch between Gonzales and our house. The first leg was three and a half miles of blacktop, Highway 90A (the road going from Gonzales to San Antonio). This road has not changed much in the past sixty years.

The second leg was the Greenwood Road, an all-weather county road topped with gravel. The gravel was more like river rock (large, rounded stones). Blackie never had shock absorbers, and her springs didn't function, which made the ride comparable to one in a mule-driven wagon. The noise made it impossible to carry on a normal conversation, so we often rode in silence.

The third leg of the journey, from the Greenwood Road to our house, was a quarter-mile dirt road. The soil was a gummy clay. During rainy times, it was nearly impossible for Blackie to negotiate the mudholes. Henry Ford, again with his genius, designed the Model A for difficult terrain. Our road was a real test of Mr. Ford's product. The car rode high off the ground and had a geared-down transmission (its low gear much like that of a tractor's). The skinny tires sometimes sank several inches into the muddy ruts.

When the mud was at its worst, Brother and I would get out and stand on the back bumper to provide more weight on the rear tires. Once Mom even had to get out and stand on the bumper while Brother and I pushed. Sis stayed in the car; she didn't weigh enough to make any difference. When the added weight on the back and the pushing didn't work, Mike and Tobe, our mule team, would have to rescue us. After one episode, Dad spoke with the

Precinct 4 County Commissioner. He provided us with several loads of gravel for the worst spots. That solved our mudhole problems. He had our vote and support for the rest of his political career.

I don't remember ever having a flat tire while we were out on the road. But from time to time, we would discover a flat while Blackie was garaged. "That's not too bad," Dad would say. "It's only flat on the bottom." We always had a tire-patching kit on hand. I called it a "monkey patch" because it had a picture of a monkey on the front. I never understood the connection between monkeys and tire patches. (It may have been the Monkey Grip Patch brand, which is still available today.) The name was effective, however, because I still remember it sixty years later. The patch worked, too. I used the kit often on my bike's inner tubes. You had to prep the surface around the damaged area where the patch was to be placed. The lid of the kit had small, elevated metal holes like a cheese grater. You rubbed the damaged area with this lid, making the surface more receptive to the glue. The patch stayed secure under the air pressure of the tire and the weight of the car or bike.

I became proficient with tire patches. Because I liked to ride my bike in the woods, I often picked up mesquite thorns that pierced the tires. One Christmas, I got a set of brand new tires, complete with tubes. It was my favorite gift that year.

Our five-mile trip into town on Saturday afternoon to barter for staple goods was always an adventure. I wouldn't have used the term "adventure" back then to describe the ride, but that's really what it was. Brother, Sis and I shared the back seat with 60 dozen eggs and a water can. We had to fill the leaky radiator with water about every five miles. Blackie had only one window, which was on the driver's side, so there was nothing to block the wind and cold. To stay warm, Sis and I shared one of Mom's homemade quilts (Brother had his own). In forty-degree, rainy weather, it could be a long, miserable ride. Regardless of the wind velocity or intensity of the blowing rain, Mom's triangle scarf always seemed to keep her pin curls neatly in place. The four pounds of butter she carried into town to trade stayed firmly on her lap. The interior of our two-door sedan had just enough room for four people, and there were five of us.

Blackie's cruising speed was about thirty miles per hour. At that speed, Dad's old belt that held the driver's-side door closed strained under the pressure. I never knew exactly how fast we went because the speedometer was erratic. On cold days, I wished we would go faster so we could shorten our misery. On the other hand, with increased speed, the wind flow increased proportionately through the three open windows, which dropped the temperature in the cabin. This could well have been the discovery of the windchill factor.

On the trip home on Saturday afternoon, we usually had a twenty-five-pound block of ice secured to the floppy rear bumper. On a 100-degree summer day, driving five miles home at slow speeds reduced the block to about fifteen pounds. But it was enough ice for tea on Saturday, Sunday and sometimes Monday.

All in all, Blackie had some redeeming qualities. She always managed to get us where we were going, and we always survived the ride.

Not pretty, but reliable.

World War II

When the threat of war came in the late thirties, our nation was tired and depleted. The Depression had taken its toll—we were already fighting to survive. Everyone prayed that war could be averted, even as Hitler was ravaging Europe. It had been only twenty years since World War I had ended. That war was supposed to have been "the war to end all wars." The dreaded thought that the sons of the men who had died in World War I would be called to fight was unbearable. But that fear became a reality December 7, 1941, at Pearl Harbor.

I was only five when the United States entered the war, but I remember that the radio was an important source of information. Because our radio was battery-operated, we used it almost exclusively for war news. The two radio war correspondents I remember were Edward R. Murrow and H.V. Kaltenborn. Their voices resonated throughout the country as they provided eyewitness accounts of the action during the height of the European battles in late '43 and '44. In late 1944, when we had electrical outlets installed, we bought a second-hand, electric radio. We could then listen to FDR's fireside chats. His frequent reports on the progress of the war and the condition of our country united us all and continued to give strength to the families in our community.

The Movie Tone Newsreels shown between features at the Crystal Theater provided graphic pictures of battle scenes and the suffering victims in the war-torn countries. The Schraders could seldom afford to attend movies, but those people who did shared the experience with us.

In addition to radio and newsreels, local newspapers were a tremendous source of information during these years. We read the accounts of Robert Trout, Ernie Pyle and Andy Rooney who reported from the front lines. During one three-month period in the fall of 1943, only one front-page headline in the *Gonzales Inquirer* pertained to something other than the war: "Apaches Beat Seguin" (football). I suppose the editor felt the readers needed a short break from the grim war news, and Texas high school football had always been important to our town.

Newspapers also served as a marketing tool to promote the sale of war bonds to help pay for the war. Our country was already deeply in debt because of the Depression. The *Inquirer* led the local war-bond drive by creating competition among the communities in the county. A headline in the fall of 1943 encouraged this rivalry by stating that Gonzales had achieved 50 percent of its goal. A few days later the headline said that Nixon had exceeded its goal! Shortly after that, the paper reported that Gonzales had reached its goal too. Another edition told us that Gonzales County school children had bought several thousand dollars in war bonds and stamps. A war stamp sold for as little as twenty-five cents. Although a quarter, for many students, was hard to come by, it was a great return on the investment.

By far, the best source of information about war conditions came from the families of the servicemen. Letters from the men and women overseas were shared with friends and neighbors, and the news spread rapidly throughout the community. There were dramatic, gut-wrenching stories from the battlefront. Occasionally, we would see a letter from a serviceman in a German POW camp. The correspondence normally took about four months to arrive home, but it played a vital role in bringing hope to the loved ones who watched and waited.

One vivid memory I have of the war years was rationing. We had to sacrifice many daily necessities in order to win the war, and the way the country came together was amazing. The Emergency Price Control Act of 1942 set the rationing wheels in motion. A ration board was established in Gonzales County and was staffed with many local volunteers. Everything from gasoline to sliced bread was regulated. Our family was issued an "A" sticker for gasoline, which meant we didn't need fuel for our business and we didn't have a direct connection to the war effort. Our "A" sticker allowed us three gallons of gas a week. Demand for rubber for the war meant we couldn't buy tires, and the government also placed a ban on recapping them. So Blackie spent many days cozily ensconced in the garage, and we made fewer trips to town.

Our local grocery store collected our unused cooking fat—it contained glycerin that was used in making black gunpowder. Used nylon stockings were collected to make parachutes. Our elementary school had an ongoing tin-can drive. I always hunted old, rusty tin cans when I went out to play, and I remember how impressed I was with the huge piles of cans and old scrap metal that accumulated on the school grounds.

Many citizens in Gonzales planted victory gardens. This helped meet the demand for fresh vegetables, and it lessened the demand for canned goods and tin cans. Living on the farm during these difficult years became a definite advantage: we always had plenty of milk, eggs, butter and bacon. Mom did her part to eliminate sugar in her baking: she used lots of homemade molasses. She and Dad even stopped drinking coffee. Eventually our ration books consisted of red and blue stamps representing a certain number of points. The scarcest products were assigned the largest number of points. If an item, such as meat, came into short supply, the point value rose. Mom kept the family books, so she kept track of the point value of the coupons. At the time, I didn't pay much attention to her coupon book—I just knew it was worth its weight in gold and no one used it but Mom.

The black market was rampant during this time. We even heard rumors in Gonzales that a farmer was raising chickens to sell on the black market. Dad scorned the practice and insisted that if any item wasn't available through legitimate channels, we would "do without." This was hard on me: I was addicted to bubble gum and considered it a necessity. Before long, bubble gum became almost impossible to find, a fact that helped me learn to "do without."

In the early forties, the Schrader family would occasionally attend a Saturday night dance. It was a pleasant social event for the entire family. Early one Saturday evening, Dad announced we would no longer be attending the dances. Disappointed, we asked why. He said he didn't feel right going to dance while "our boys were fighting and dying." Instead we would visit the families who had soldiers in combat. They needed our support more than we needed to dance. We made the visits a number of times, and I asked only once if I had to go. The answer was quick and firm: of course, I had to. My parents knew the experience would help me appreciate the sacrifices that were being made. It did. We had little to share with these families when we made our visits—but Mom always took a fresh fruit pie or her homemade kolaches (Czech pastries). When I heard the brokenhearted families crying and saying over and over, "Our son is not coming home," I would take a walk or wait in the car.

As a seven-year-old, it was hard for me to understand why Americans were dying in other countries. Once I asked Mom for an explanation. She said that Americans would rather die than become slaves and that our soldiers were protecting us from slavery. We were born free. God gave us freedom, but two men were trying to take it from us. One in Germany named Hitler and the other in Japan named Tojo wanted to rule the world. Mom showed me on a map that America was located between these two countries. She then showed me graphic pictures in a *Life* magazine she had borrowed from a neighbor. I saw images of dead soldiers on the battlefields and starving people in the concentration camps. Mom shared the conversation she had with a mother who had recently lost her nineteen-year-old son. She said her friend was getting better and she was going to survive the tragedy. She asked Mom for one favor: "Every time you pray, thank God for what my son did for our country." No doubt Mom did.

Soon after that, I told Mom and Dad that I learned in Sunday school that you should not hate anyone, but I couldn't help it, I hated the Germans and the Japanese. Dad responded by saying he didn't hate all Germans and Japanese, but he did hate Hitler and Tojo. His honest answer made me feel better.

Many young men on the front lines were members of Company K, a Texas National Guard unit activated in the Gonzales area in 1940. This company, part of the 141st Infantry Regiment, hit the beaches of Salerno, Italy, in September 1943. It turned out to be one of the bloodiest and costliest battles in the European theater. Shortly after Company K landed, the grim reports began to reach Gonzales County. The difficulties in our daily lives became minor compared to the sorrow we felt for these fighting men and their families. The fear and horror experienced by the fighters' families was relentless. When word came that another boy was killed, the question dug deep into the hearts of the parents and wives, "Is my son (or my husband) going to be next?"

One of our neighbors, Louis Mudd, lost his brother Christmas Day 1943. To add to the grief and pain, another brother continued in battle with Company K. He was fortunate enough to make it home.

I was once awakened in the middle of the night by voices from the living room. My parents' closest friends had two sons in battle. They had learned the day before that another local boy had died in combat. He was a schoolmate of their younger son. All four parents talked quietly and wept—then they prayed. I crawled back in bed and, for once, appreciated having my big brother asleep at my side.

To give recognition and support to the families whose loved ones were serving in the military, the war department provided banners that could be displayed in the windows of their homes. The banners, about the size of a standard window pane, were red, white and blue and laced with gold-braided cord. There was a star for every member of the family in the service. A gold star indicated a fallen hero. As neighbors passed the homes displaying the banners, they paused, said a prayer and gave respect to the family. Brother commented that one day we might have a banner in our window. I'm sure that sent chills down my folks' spine.

One member of Company K was Sonny Tuch. Sonny knew a thing or two about survival from living in the Depression. He had lost his mother when he was four years old, and shortly afterward his father disappeared. He was raised by his grandfather until he was seventeen. His grandfather's main source of income consisted of odd jobs such as cutting and delivering firewood for a dollar a cord. (A cord is a lot of wood, particularly when you cut it with an ax.) In 1938, fifteen days before he was fifteen years old, Sonny joined Company K. He needed the dollar a week that the Guard paid, and he also thought this would be an opportunity for an adventure. Little did he know how his life would change two years later.

The recruiter who signed up Sonny waived the standard weight requirement of 120 pounds, reasoning that Sonny would eventually meet that minimum. During Sonny's first training meeting, the commanding officer, while inspecting the troop line, stepped in front of recruit Tuch and ordered: "Sonny boy, get into the kitchen and stay there." Sonny obeyed half the order: he went to the kitchen but he didn't stay for long. He talked his way out of the kitchen and into the field "where the real men were and where the action was." A thirty-five-mile hike with a full pack on his back did not discourage the less-than-120-pound trooper. He was on his way to becoming a true leader.

Sonny shipped out with Company K and fought alongside his buddies at Salerno. The 141st Infantry was not only the first to land in Europe but also the first of the Seventh Army to cross the Moselle River in France and the first of the 36th Division to enter Germany. Unlike many of his friends, Sonny lived to tell about it.

One story he told was how he and fourteen other American soldiers were holed up in a German wine cellar. Periodically, the Nazis would run down the stairs, spraying the cellar with small-arms fire. Sonny surmised that the Krauts didn't have hand grenades or they certainly would have used them. The GIs held off the Germans for three days. Then abruptly the Germans departed, apparently deciding they had killed all the Americans. Only four of the Americans survived. Eleven lay dead, some for three days, in the cellar. Sonny was shot twice in the hand. By some miracle, he still has full function, in spite of the blood poisoning that resulted from inadequate medical attention. The only permanent disability he suffered was a fractured eardrum.

Sonny's military duties went far beyond the job description of a tech sergeant. His officers, recognizing his leadership potential, assigned him to one of the most difficult jobs: handling soldiers suffering from battle fatigue. Many of these young men had a hard time coping with the effects of war. Sonny's comment today: "How could you blame a fighter who had given so much, who had killed, experienced so many killings, and put his life on the line so many times?" He reasons, "You treat a person good and they will start acting good." His compassion helped many GIs through this difficult period.

Today Sonny tells his stories with courage and candor, pausing at times to control his emotions. After sixty years, he still breaks up at the thought of having to avoid stepping on a fallen comrade. Many times, he says, his only hope was to live one more day. When asked if he had any regrets, his reply is simple and sincere: "I wanted to do the right thing, to make things right."

After the war, Sonny vowed he would not live as he had during the Depression. He knew it was up to him to change that, and he did. He built a successful tire business in Gonzales and bought farms and ranches in the area, including property that later produced oil. He credits his success to applying the golden rule. He had compassion and the good judgment to know how to work with people to improve their lives: "I love to help people with nothing feel like they are somebody. That is what makes people better."

After lunch one recent afternoon, Sonny told me about one of his current projects: pruning and grafting pecan trees on his farm. He projected that in ten years he would have a productive pecan orchard. Some eighty-one-year-olds never buy green bananas. But Sonny has never known limitations. At age fifteen, he was getting out of the kitchen patrol to develop his potential, and at age eighty-one, he is making sure his pecan trees produce to their potential.

Sonny represents millions of Americans who were called to war. He and the men of Company K were assigned a job, and they accepted it willingly. Their sacrifice and achievement cannot be overstated. The enemy learned the hard way that tyranny would not be tolerated in America. The Depression made Sonny stronger. Sonny, and millions like him, saved not only our country but also the world. Thank you, Sonny Tuch, for your service to mankind.

In the midst of all the war's horror and tragedy, a few amusing stories emerged. According to one, certain young women took advantage of the military system by marrying different GIs just before they were shipped out. These gals were called "Allotment Annies" because they collected a soldier's marriage allotment and even life insurance in the event the GI was killed. Our town buzzed with speculation when an attractive young woman of questionable reputation hastily married a GI who was shipped out a few days after the wedding. The rumors really became rampant when she relocated to Norfolk, Virginia, where sailors shipped out in large numbers from the naval base. That town was flooded with lonely, vulnerable GIs looking for companionship.

One young woman named Elsie, working the nightclubs in Norfolk, married six servicemen and was working on number seven when she was apprehended. Her income was $300 a month (a lot of money in those days), plus the possibility of collecting a couple of life-insurance benefits. She was caught when two sailors in an English pub began telling one another about the wife they had left behind. They pulled out their wallets and showed each other a picture of the same bride! The bad news was that the poor guys beat up each other before discovering the truth. The good news was that Elsie was brought to justice.

Many of the young men and women returning home from the war had no marketable skills. The GI Bill provided the opportunity for thousands to obtain a college education or develop skills in a trade school. It was an investment that helped spur an economic expansion unlike any in the history of the world. These soldiers had looked death in the eye and in that process had developed the confidence to succeed. The Depression boys won the war, put the horrors behind them and, in a few short years, elevated the standard of living in the country to heights no one could have ever imagined. They were, as Tom Brokaw called them, the "Greatest Generation."

Casualty List

Gonzales County

Seventy-four brave young men from Gonzales County gave their lives so that the rest of us could live in freedom. I will always be grateful to them and their families for their sacrifice, and I will never forget how fragile life was back then.

Name	Rank	Hometown
Lester A. Bailey	CPL	Gonzales
Joy V. Baker	PVT	Leesville
Edmund W. Bielefeld	PFC	Cost
John B. Blackmon	PFC	Gonzales
Laval D. Brown, Jr.	SSGT	Gonzales
Paulie C. Buss	SGT	Gonzales
Glenn E. Campbell	2nd. Lt.	Gonzales
Leslie M. Caraway	SSGT	Gonzales
James. R. Collins, Jr.	2nd. Lt.	Gonzales
Clyde C. Crozier	SSGT	Gonzales

Earl Daniels	SGT	Gonzales
Felix Delgado	PFC	Gonzales
Horace K. Duncan	1st. Lt.	Gonzales
Raymond H. Ehrig	SSGT	Gonzales
Robert C. Farmer	2nd. Lt.	Gonzales
Frank U. Flores	SGT	Gonzales
Lawrence W. Floyd	SSGT	Gonzales
Humbert Martinez Galindo	PVT	Gonzales
Martin P. Garcia	PFC	Gonzales
Guy D. Glass	SGT	Gonzales
C.P. Goodwin, Jr.	1st. Lt.	Gonzales
J.J. Halliburton	TSGT	Gonzales
Harper W. Harris	CPL	Gonzales
James A. M. Helms	SGT	Gonzales
Clyde S. Henley	1st. Sgt.	Gonzales
Arthur W. Hunter	CPL	Gonzales
Lynwood Logan	2nd. Lt.	Gonzales
David Pruett Mahan		Nixon
Henry W. Malatek	CPL	Gonzales
Jack W. Mang	PFC	Gonzales
Frank G. Martin	SGT	Gonzales
Felipe C. Martinez	PFC	Gonzales
Victor I. May	SSGT	Gonzales
Braxton McKinney	PFC	Gonzales
Quillian G. McMichen	SGT	Gonzales
Huey Irvin Mercer	Fireman 3c	Gonzales
James L. Miller	SGT	Gonzales
Roy Mudd		Gonzales
Chester R. Nagel	SGT	Gonzales
James E. Newberry, Jr.	2nd. Lt.	Gonzales
Henry P. Olivarez	PFC	Gonzales
David K. Ollre	SSGT	Gonzales
Charles Darnell Parker	Seaman 2c	Waelder
James Wayne Patteson	Phar M. 2c	Nixon
Boyce Penrod, Jr.	Capt.	Gonzales
Adolf Petrach		Gonzales
Frank Petras	PVT	Gonzales

Joseph N. Phelps	F1 0	Gonzales
Richard A. Polasek	PVT	Gonzales
Elidio A. Quintero	PFC	Waelder
Robert S. Rentz	PVT	Gonzales
John B. Rightmer	SGT	Gonzales
Chester T. Robinson	PVT	Gonzales
Vidal M. Salaz	PFC	Gonzales
Louie Schellenberg	PFC	Gonzales
James H. Scholl	2nd. Lt.	Gonzales
Edward H. Sellers	SGT	Gonzales
Marlin J. Sessions	PFC	Bebe
Horace L. Sherry	PFC	Gonzales
Agle Davis Shipley	Seaman 2c	Nixon
Cruz Soto	PVT	Gonzales
Juan Soto	PFC	Nixon
Carl E. Spieckermann	1st Lt.	Gonzales
Marvin M. Spieckermann	PVT	Gonzales
Henry J. Stehle	PVT	Gonzales
Jack K. Swearingen	SSGT	Gonzales
Juan H. Tovar	PFC	Gonzales
Lee C. Trevino	PVT	Gonzales
Ignacio G. Vasquez	PFC	Gonzales
Joe M. Velasquez	PFC	Waelder
Charlie J. Vlasak	PVT	Gonzales
Louis F. Wagner	PFC	Gonzales
Calvin W. Warren	SSGT	Gonzales
Fred West	PFC	Gonzales

Source: Texas Military Forces Museum, Camp Mabry, Austin.

SHOWN IN PHOTOGRAPH

First Row: C. R. Smith, J. J. Mikesh, R. H. Ehrig, J. J. Bruns, D. Howell, O. Howell, E. R. Chumchal, D. D. Glasco, O. C. Bailey, E. C. Chumchal, H. C. Jowers, A. E. Speed.

Second Row: C. E. Tuch, J. F. Broz, O. A. B. Hoerig, Jr., A. F. Malatek, R. F. Richter, J. L. Mills, H. P. Ehrig, F. J. Petras, W. W. Talley, H. L. Wolff, J. L. Broz, B. J. Robinson.

Third Row: J. H. Robinson, J. Broz, F. C. Richter, C. C. Bailey, C. Petras, G. L. Hoy, C. O. Mudd, L. J. Drozd, J. G. Smith, E. H. Boysen, R. D. Tuch, V. Mikes, R. J. Tomas.

SHOWN IN PHOTOGRAPH

First Row: B. O. Ehrig, G. E. Ebel, W. J. Ronshausen, S. E. Andrews, J. C. Nesloney, J. P. Heil, R. F. Gerloff, V. A. Gerloff, I. F. Smith, O. A. Ehrig, J. L. Shock.

Second Row: L. A. Bailey, A. W. Wolff, H. W. Malatek, R. B. Van Beveran, W. R. Miller, D. U. Mills, J. W. Houston, L. F. Knippa, P. D. Crow, R. Mikes, A. Schobey.

Third Row: J. B. Rightmer, R. C. Crow, E. Mikesh, J. E. Cavasar, L. J. Kimber, H. C. Heil, R. A. Polasek, C. E. Hunter, L. P. Bush, M. Havel, A. F. Ehrig, R. R. Gerold.

Company K, 141st Infantry, Gonzales.

King Cotton

Today when visitors drive through the quaint, narrow streets of Gonzales, they go back in time to the days when cotton was king. Many of the antebellum homes along the tree-lined streets were built by prosperous cotton growers in the mid-1800s. Gonzales had the right growing conditions for this yearly crop of "white gold." It was the main source of income for the Schrader family.

Every April our mules, Mike and Tobe, pulled Dad on the cotton planter, a cumbersome device that drilled the holes, deposited the seeds and covered up the holes with soil. About three-fourths a bushel per acre assured a good stand. Planting the cotton took only a few days. After that we waited and waited—and prayed for rain.

The rains were critical. Too much would knock the delicate cotton blooms off the stalk. Heavy rains could also whack the mature cotton right out of the bolls. So we prayed for gentle, spring rain—and God blessed us many times over.

When the plants grew to three or four inches in height, we thinned them to eliminate the weaker ones and ensure the maximum yield. In the process, weeds were removed and the soil was loosened so the young plants could breathe. This was known as "chopping cotton." The chopping was done with a hoe and can only be described as backbreaking labor.

When Brother got a driver's license and worked away from the farm in the summers, Dad and I were left to do the chopping. At the time, I thought this was one of the worst jobs on the farm. But, upon reflection, I cherish the hours spent listening to my father talk about his deep religious faith, his commitment to Mom and the family, and the value of an education.

Once in conversation, I asked Dad if he was ever really scared. “In 1935,” he responded, “when your brother was six and your sister was a baby, we were in the middle of the Depression. The Guadalupe had flooded and we made about half a crop. A full crop would have given us little more than we barely needed to get by. It was a tough year.” He paused and then continued: “In June of 1936, one week after you were born, the Guadalupe did it again. This time it was about an 80 percent loss. In the spring of 1937, when I was getting ready for another growing season, I was sure afraid! I didn’t know what we would have done if we had another crop failure. Thank God we didn’t.” I think Dad had a reason to tell me that story: he didn’t want me to be a farmer. He wanted me to pursue my education and have more options in life than he had known. I will always be grateful to him for that.

I never understood why cotton required so much attention. But like a lot of things on the farm, I had more questions than there were answers. We cultivated the soil often until the delicate plants grew to the blooming stage. We had two kinds of cultivators: a riding cultivator pulled by our mules and a walking cultivator. Dad taught me to use the walking cultivator. With practice, I got so proficient that I could slip between the stalks and zap a cocklebur. Dad would work beside me on the riding cultivator. I insisted he ride—it was my way of proving myself.

On exceptionally hot days, Dad and I would each consume at least a gallon of water. We brought it to the field in glass jugs wrapped with moist grass sacks to keep it cool. At quitting time, all I could think about was going home and drawing a bucket of that wonderful, cool well water. One day after working the field, I drew a bucket and was bringing it to my mouth when I noticed a bird deposit. Cupping the water with both hands, I disposed of the debris and enthusiastically drank the rest. From then on, I made it a point to turn the bucket upside down when it wasn't being used.

By August the cotton had burst out of the bolls and was ready to be picked. The work involved in harvesting explains why people use the term "cotton picking" at times when they need a descriptive expletive. "Keep your 'cotton-picking' hands off that!" As a boy, I learned firsthand how the phrase evolved. For starters, cotton picking took place during the hottest time of year. Picking was done by hand from one of two positions: on your knees, or standing bent at your waist. You picked the cotton off the stalk and dropped it in a long sack slung over your shoulder. The more you picked, the heavier the sack became. Your shoulders and back ached under the sack's weight as you dragged it along. As you picked the cotton, the sharp, pointed ends of the dry bolls pricked your fingertips, making them swell. Work gloves were useless; you needed the dexterity of bare fingers for picking. I surmise that the best pickers developed calluses on their hands and fingertips; that's why they were able to pick long after the rest of us had to retire and nurse our wounds.

In August of 1940, when I was four, our cotton was ready to be harvested. Dad told Brother to go about a mile across the pasture and tell our black neighbor that cotton picking would begin the next morning. Much to Brother's chagrin, I wanted to tag along. Mom told him to let me go.

We arrived at the neighbor's house, and the scene was one I will never forget. The house was a shack. Three or four skinny, dirty kids were standing in front, staring at us with a look of despair. One girl, who was older than the others, stood naked and totally uninhibited. Hanging in a tree next to the house was a skinned jackrabbit covered with flies. This was their supper. Two hounds slept in the shade under the house. They were so thin they could hardly walk, much less chase down a rabbit. Although I was only four, I knew this family lived at the brink of death. As we walked home, I asked Brother, "Why are they so poor?" Brother didn't have an answer for my foolish question. He too was saddened. We walked home in silence.

The next morning, just after dawn, the neighbor's entire family was in our front yard ready to start picking. They had to wait a couple of hours for the dew to evaporate from the bolls. Dad gave everyone a sack, and they left for the cotton field. The kids did not need to be motivated or disciplined; they knew this was about their survival.

After finishing his chores, Dad drove the wagon to the field so the workers would have a place to empty their sacks after they were full. I watched as the family picked in silence at a steady pace, stopping occasionally to quench their thirst. The only time I saw smiles on their faces was at the sight of Mom coming from the house carrying a basket of sandwiches. I could always smell that homemade bread a mile away. I often wondered if this was the only meal this family would have until the next day.

The family worked twelve-hour days every day until all the cotton was harvested. The sharp bolls snagged what little clothing they wore, and they were covered with dirt from the field. I wondered how they could recover overnight and be back in the field again the next day. I admired them for their tenacity and pitied them for their lot in life.

Years later, I decided to really get serious about picking cotton. My plan was to make enough money to upgrade my wardrobe in anticipation of the new school year. Mom made a custom-fit picking sack for me out of heavy-duty duck. The sack was five feet long, and the shoulder strap was long enough for my hands to flow freely from the cotton bolls to the sack. At full capacity, the sack was easy to manage and large enough that I didn't have to spend a lot of time weighing in. Mom made knee pads for me from the leftover duck and stuffed them tightly with sewing material scraps. Each pad had four straps—two on the top and two on the bottom, triple-stitched for maximum strength. The pads covered my knees, and the straps looped around my legs.

Dad paid our best pickers $1.60 per hundred pounds. I was just another picker—he didn't believe in nepotism. I started the day full of enthusiasm and came home exhausted—and short of my goal. I kept trying, but I soon realized that I couldn't pick a hundred pounds a day, even on my best days. Even if I could, that would bring in only $1.60 per day. My performance level dropped rapidly. Dad graciously let me off the hook, and I looked for other ways to become an entrepreneur.

During the peak of the harvest season, Dad took cotton to the gin two or three times a week. The ten-mile round trip to Gonzales by mule team and wagon took about three hours. About half of that time was spent waiting in line at the gin behind the wagons of other farmers. I liked to go with Dad. The ride to the gin was fun—sitting high on top of the fluffy, white load, enjoying the cool of the morning. Returning home was not so pleasant. By that time of day, the August heat was beating down upon us.

On one trip home, after receiving a handsome check for his bale of cotton, Dad bought five or six Milky Way candy bars. One was for me to enjoy, and the rest were for the family. Sitting in the back of the wagon on the empty floor, I was overcome with temptation. The hot sun was turning the chocolate-covered bars into chocolate sauce. To avoid further damage and possible loss of all the candy,

I figured I had better eat as many as possible before the damage became irreversible.

I guess my digestive system wasn't programmed for store-bought candy. The chuckholes in the Greenwood Road leading to our house and the blistering heat combined to give me a whale of a bellyache. Dad looked over his shoulder to see me curled in a fetal position, my mouth and my bib overalls covered in gooey chocolate. I got no sympathy from him—nor any from Mom when we got home and she learned what I had done. To this day, I'm not much of a chocolate lover.

In 1949, when I turned thirteen, Dad wanted me to transport the cotton pickers back and forth from the field by car. I had already been testing my driving expertise by cruising out in the pasture. Mom was definitely not in favor of the idea, but Dad prevailed. I was excited about the prospect because I was a good driver—heck, I hadn't had one wreck. As my final test, I took a ride with Dad up the Greenwood Road. I drove. Roads tend to have different boundaries than pastures, and I had some difficulty maneuvering the car at thirty miles an hour. As we approached the home of a neighbor, I turned to Dad to ask why this couple lived together and weren't married. As Dad began to explain to me about lack of commitment, I took their mailbox out of commission, post and all. The replacement cost me a month's allowance. Mom didn't say, "I told you so." But I knew what she was thinking.

Some days Dad didn't get home from the gin by the pickers' quitting time. So Mom, wearing her flowered bonnet, would walk to the field and help me with the weigh-in. The pickers would hoist their full sacks of cotton on the scale, hook the strap on the scale's hook and make sure the sack was not touching the ground. I would operate the scale, sliding the weight along the balance arm. Mom would record the result in the log book.

Many cotton pickers were illiterate; they had to trust the farmer. They had no choice—they couldn't read the scale. Dad had an innate sense of fairness, and workers in the community knew they never had to question his honesty. Dad told me to always add a couple of pounds to each sack to be sure the pickers were never shorted. A family of five could work all week and still take home less than twenty-five dollars.

At the cotton gin, the cotton went through a process that removed the dirt and debris, separated the lint from the seed and baled the cotton fibers. A 1,500-pound load resulted in a 500-pound bale and approximately 1,000 pounds of seed. The gin operators kept a portion of the seed to cover the ginning fee and bought the balance. The seed went next door to a cottonseed processing plant, where it was made into products such as cottonseed oil and cottonseed cake, a highly nutritious food for livestock.

The final step was selling the cotton bales. This was where the farmer realized the earnings from a year of hard labor. The cotton buyer came to Gonzales from Houston. I never did know his name, but I will never forget the way he looked. He was a heavyset, balding man with suspenders that cut deep into the flesh visible under his sweat-soaked white shirt. He constantly chewed on an old cigar that fit perfectly into the space where a front tooth should have been. His helper, a thin, jittery fellow, took a sample from Dad's bale by slicing into the bale with a large knife. He wrapped the cotton sample in butcher paper and took it in to the buyer. Using a magnifying glass, the buyer meticulously examined the length of the staple (cotton fiber) while Dad nervously waited.

There was no competitive bidding on the load. There was no verification of the bale's weight. The price was determined right then and there, by one man. A good year for the Schraders was ten bales, and the average price was $100 per bale. Dad never smiled as he walked away from the buyer's shack with that check in his hand—but his face showed relief. The weight of the world was finally off his shoulders. We made it through the season and with God's grace would be back again the next year.

Mule-driven seed planter for cotton, corn and maize.

There was nothing glamorous about picking cotton.

Waiting at the gin: during peak harvesting time, the wait could be more than three hours.

Hog Butchering Day

The year was 1944. I was eight years old, weighed sixty pounds and had a wiry build, but I could single-handedly butcher a 400-pound hog. Or so I thought. In reflecting on the entire process, I marvel that my dad, Grandpa Vackar and one neighbor were physically able to complete this arduous task.

Hogs are prolific animals. The gestation period is three months, three weeks and three days (or approximately 120 days). A litter averages six to eight babies. On occasion, we hit the jackpot with twelve.

All of our male shoats (young pigs) were castrated. After that unfortunate experience, they normally had a growing spurt—another one of nature's mysteries. Our boar used for breeding was never butchered. Boar's meat has a strong taste and a slight smell. We shipped the boars off to the auction on a regular basis to avoid in-breeding.

Hog raising was an economical enterprise for a Depression family. The animals were low maintenance: hearty, seldom sick, confined in a pen and small enough to be controlled. The mortality rate was low. The major cause of death was a sow rolling over onto one of her piglets.

Hogs' primary food was corn produced on the farm. They also ate slop, which was any foodstuff our family didn't eat. Potato peelings, the snap ends of peas and beans, leaves from vegetables such as turnips and beets became slop. There wasn't much a hog wouldn't eat. They ate so fast, I doubt they knew what they were eating and, apparently, didn't care. Even dishwater went into the slop can. (The lye soap we used to wash the dishes never seemed to adversely affect the hogs.) The milk the family did not consume became slop, and we had an abundance of milk. Two cows were milked twice a day, leaving them only enough to satisfy their growing calves. As the calves grew, they required more milk, which meant less for the hogs. Seasonal variations like this weakened the slop from time to time, so we would supplement the hogs' diet by buying "shorts" at the feed store. Funny name, but that's what they were called. They consisted of wheat, chaff and other unknown ingredients, but they added nutritional strength.

We butchered hogs to provide our supply of pork. By mid-summer every year, we had eaten the last of the sausage, and any remaining bacon and ham were beginning to take on a rancid taste. The pantry was becoming too hot to store any pork products. Hog butchering usually took place in the fall when the first big norther arrived. A norther is a fast-moving cold front that makes temperatures fall and often brings rain and a spell of cool weather.

Hog butchering was not for the faint-of-heart. Mom refused to be involved, especially in the early stages, which began with a well-placed .22 bullet between the animal's eyes. Dad was an expert shot; the hog went down instantly. Dad drained the blood from its neck right away to prevent the development of bacteria and to save the blood for blood sausage. Grandpa Vackar was the only person that professed to like blood sausage. Why, I'll never know. As a growing boy in the Depression, I would eat anything—well, almost anything. I couldn't handle blood sausage.

After phase one was completed, a mule-drawn skid was pulled near the entrance to the pens. It took every available ounce of manpower to roll the hog onto the skid. We were dealing with a large, bulky specimen. If it was a brood sow that had lost her reproductive ability, she could weigh more than 400 pounds.

Tobe pulled the skid up the hill to a staging area where we had two wash pots of boiling water. Next to the wash pots was a fifty-five-gallon drum, tilted at a forty-five-degree angle. We pulled the skid up as close as possible to the opening of the drum. With all available muscle, we pushed the animal into the drum and filled it with hot water. After soaking for a few minutes, the animal was pulled up and turned around to soak the other side. This process prepared the skin for shaving. We removed the hog from the drum and returned it to the skid. The staff, armed with sharp butcher knives, began removing the hair from the entire surface of the animal. As the shaving progressed, grass sacks boiled in the wash pots. The sacks were used to condition the skin to make hair removal easier, similar to a man using a hot, damp towel to soften his beard. The hot grass sacks helped in the hard-to-shave areas such as the neck, face, head and feet. These areas required slow, close work. Shaving the ears was difficult, but it had to be done right. The ears went into tamales, and were our neighbor's payment for his hard work. The feet also had to be left without a single hair. Not too appetizing looking at pig's hair while you're eating pig's feet.

After the shaving was completed, slits were made in the lower ankle between the Achilles' tendon and the main ankle area. Into these slits we inserted hooks attached to ropes that were on a pulley. We tied the pulley to a large limb of a substantial mesquite tree. Then Dad and Grandpa pulled the shaven hog upward until the nose was just off the ground. The main butchering process could now begin.

The underside of the hog was opened from the top to the bottom. To avoid contamination, the descending colon, near the rear orifice, was tied off with butcher twine. The liver was saved and the kidneys were set aside to be put into blood sausage. My after-school job was to carry off what was left of the internal parts. By then, there wasn't much except the stomach and the large intestines. I was afraid that a wolf, coyote or some other wild animal would ambush me as I was toting the bloody remains to the pasture. Fortunately, that never occurred.

The next step was to wash the entire carcass with cold water. The head was removed and the carcass split down the middle of the backbone from tip to tip using a hand saw. Dad tied a short rope to the hook that was in the slit, and Grandpa released the pulley, lowering a half carcass onto Dad's back. Dad carried the carcass up the hill to the smokehouse. Forty yards was a long way to carry a 150-pound side. The process was repeated for the other half. Dad had an amazingly strong back.

The selected cuts of a hog are bacon, ham and chops. The bacon comes from the sides and the upper belly. The ham comes from the rump, and the chops from the upper back. We set aside the remaining lean meat for sausage. The underbelly, mostly fat, was rendered for lard. Some dry salt belly came from this area also.

The bacon slabs and hams were carefully trimmed of excess fat. Then they had to be cured. The curing process consisted of rubbing down the meat twice a day for a week, using a dry-rub compound. The dry rub was Dad's secret recipe. It consisted of brown sugar, salt, garlic salt, black pepper and other spices that he refused to divulge. We hung the meat from the ceiling of the smokehouse and smoked it for two days and one night. Dad had to get out of bed several times during that night to keep the fire stoked and continuously smoking.

Dad's famous sausage was made by mixing the lean meat with the fat. The ratio of lean to fat was a critical element in making superior sausage. Too much lean would sacrifice flavor, texture and moisture. Too much fat would sacrifice substance—that is, the fat would cook away and the sausage would have a mealy texture. Too much fat with the dry sausage would result in a fat coating inside your mouth. Dad never documented the formula for the ratio because it was impossible to do. The recipe had been passed down through generations of Schraders. The same went for seasoning—never measurable but always just right. The spices were salt, black and red pepper and garlic—no sage or saltpeter.

For the sausage casing, we used the small intestines. They were thoroughly washed and soaked in salt water before stuffing. The hog didn't have enough small intestines for all the sausage casing we needed, so we bought additional casing at the meat market in Gonzales.

The sausage was processed in two ways. Half was smoked for only one night, then cut into three-inch pieces, covered with hog lard and stored in crocks. The other half was thoroughly smoked and became dry sausage that could be eaten cooked or uncooked.

Dad's sausage had a great reputation in the community. He sold some at the grocery store and gave some to friends and relatives. Reverend Loeske, our Lutheran pastor, always got a couple of links. I can't prove it, but I think in return he gave us a little extra divine guidance.

After the bacon and ham were fully cured, they were sliced, covered with lard and stored in crocks. The fatty area under the neck, known as the jowls, was salted down, dried out and appropriately named "dry salt jowls." Mom used this to season cooked vegetables. It was a great flavor enhancer. The rest of the fat and skin was cut into small cubes. The lard was rendered from the cubes by boiling them in the wash pot. The rendering was complete when the cracklings (fried skin) floated to the top, indicating the fat was extracted from the skin and the lard was adequately cooked. The lard was then strained into a five-gallon container, and the cracklings were likewise put into a metal container to be used later for lye soap and crackling cornbread. The fresh cracklings were a gourmet delight. Often they were cooking when we came home from school. We fished them out of the wash pot, let them cool, and ate them like potato chips.

The balance of the carcass consisted of the tail, backbone, knuckles and spareribs. The spareribs were cooked separately—they were special. The preparation process was simple: boil them with salt and pepper and serve with mustard and sauerkraut (optional). There was always some argument about who would get the tail. It was more of a novelty than anything else because it consisted mostly of fat. The backbone was boiled until all the meat fell off the bone. The resulting broth was saved and used to make red-eye gravy. Our poor dogs got some great flavored bones but no meat. When the bones were lifted from the pot, they were slick and shiny.

All the family worked well into the evening on hog butchering day. One cold November night, after an exhausting day, Grandpa Vackar brought out his homemade red wine and poured three glasses. "Who's that for?" asked Mom, pointing to the smallest glass. "It's for Buddy," Grandpa quickly replied. (Even at nine years old, I was enjoying this exchange.) "You know he's too young to drink," said Mom. It was then that Grandpa began to explain why I deserved a few sips of his home brew. "Last summer," he recalled, "Buddy climbed the live oak tree that was covered in vines, found the ripest grapes and cut them out. It was darn hard work, and I was just too tired to do it. Those grapes made the best wine I can remember. And," Grandpa continued, "Buddy did a lot of butchering today. He kept the fires going under the wash pots, helped shave the hog, cut the fat for cracklings—and carried the innards into the woods for the varmints." Mom gave in and I thoroughly enjoyed my first glass of wine. That night I slept like a baby, feeling very much like a man.

Corn: A Golden Treasure

Corn was an essential crop in the Depression. It was a basic food item for human consumption and served as feed for all our farm animals: chickens, turkeys, hogs and cows. The laborious process of delivering that crop from the field to our table helped shape my future.

Early each spring, Dad planted a few rows of corn as soon as he determined which frost was the last of the year. He had no way of knowing, of course, but he gambled for an important reason: it was a ritual for me to have roasting ears on my birthday, June 8. On the evening of "Buddy's big day," we would have a party, share supper with friends and relatives, and enjoy the first fresh corn of the season. As I recall, we cancelled a party only once because frost got the corn.

Not all corn seeds germinate after planting. So corn, like cotton, had to be planted thick to ensure a good stand. Once the young plants were up and healthy, approximately eight to twelve inches high, we would thin out the younger shoots to leave about a foot between the stalks. Good spacing was critical in producing the maximum yield, given the fertility of the soil and the prohibitive price of fertilizer.

About the time we would begin thinning the corn, we would also have to deal with the Johnsongrass. The problem had to be addressed quickly and thoroughly. A perennial noxious weed native to the Mediterranean, Johnsongrass spreads by both seed and an expanding root system. A single plant can produce more than 80,000 seeds and 200 feet of roots. This makes eradication almost impossible. But after countless hours of backbreaking labor, spread over several years, our field did become virtually free of Johnsongrass. Fortunately, because of school and homework, I could tend the cornfield only in the afternoon and on Saturday morning. Thank heaven for school.

Until the corn became too tall, we used a cultivator for tilling and weeding. Once the corn reached a height of about five and a half feet, we did the last plowing by "running the middles"—working the soil between the corn rows.

Running the middles was a downright detestable chore—it seemed to me to be an exercise in futility—undertaken in late May, when the stalks were developing roasting ears. But, like most farm practices, this one had sound reasoning behind it. Tilling the soil put fresh oxygen near the corn's roots and made the spring and summer rains more beneficial. Plowing also turned up Johnsongrass and cockleburs and kept the other weeds at bay.

In the summer of 1946, when I was ten years old, Dad thought I might be strong enough to run the middles. To make a round, I was to plow up a row, make a U-turn and plow down the adjacent row, following the mule that pulled the sweepstalk plow. Operating the tiller, I held onto the two handles that controlled the direction and the depth of the blade. The reins on the mule went over my shoulders and were tied behind my back. Managing the plow, while directing and controlling the mule, was a skill that had to be acquired. Turning the mule around at the end of the row ranked as a ten on the level of difficulty.

Tobe was particularly cantankerous that early June morning. By 10 a.m. the temperature had risen dramatically—it felt like it was 100 degrees in the field, a factor that made this job so terrible. The head-high cornstalks blocked the breeze, and the morning humidity and relentless afternoon sun created nearly oven-like conditions. To add to the aggravation, the cornstalk leaves slapped me in the face. I had no defense because both my hands had to be on the tiller. Tobe continually refused to move and then, almost as if on purpose, he bolted and pulled me head first into the brittle stalks. I recovered, sweaty and scratched—making sure Dad didn't see the tears welling up in my eyes. I continued in an erratic fashion, embarrassed for damaging the plants, knowing Dad would probably have to re-plow this row.

The truth was obvious: The job was bigger than I was. I told Dad my arms were starting to hurt and he kindly answered, "You just need more beans. Maybe you'll be ready next year." I was crushed but somewhat relieved that I was not yet man enough to run the middles.

In late June, our roasting ears reached their peak. We had corn on the cob two meals a day and canned the rest. Dad would go down the corn rows and gather the choicest ears into a cotton sack. Then we would all settle on the back porch or under the live oak tree in the backyard and help him shuck and silk. Sis would usually recruit a couple of her girlfriends to help out.

Cutting the young corn off the cob was a skill only Mom possessed. If the corn was cut too close, too much cob would be left on the kernels. Not cutting it close enough was wasteful. Mom knew all the tricks. Once the corn was removed from the cob, we scraped the cob with a knife, extracting the "milk," which added flavor and nutrition to the canned corn. This was the kids' job. I particularly liked it because Dad let me use his special Case pocketknife.

For canning, Mom used a thirty-quart pressure cooker made of heavy-duty aluminum. Inside was a removable wire rack that accommodated eighteen No. 2c cans. The bolt-down lid had a safety pop-off valve and a pressure gauge. The cans, lids and sealing tool were purchased at the hardware store. The first step was to add water to the pressure cooker until it reached a depth of four inches. The shelled corn and "milk" were spooned into each can, leaving about an inch and a half at the top, and then water was added until the level was about a half inch from the top. The cans were placed on the rack in the cooker, the lid was closed and the corn would steam for fifteen minutes. Mom would remove the cans, stir the corn inside each one, and seal the lids. The cans were again placed on the rack in the cooker and this time steamed for 105 minutes.

Some years we canned as many as sixty cans of corn! We might have processed more had we been able to afford more cans. We also canned a variety of beans and peas, all with good results. Weeks or months later, we seldom found a swollen can, which indicated a broken seal and spoilage.

After harvesting the roasting ears, we left the rest of the corn in the field to mature. These ears would be used to make cornmeal and feed the livestock. Our part during this development phase in June and July was to hope and pray for rain. Rain at this point in the growing process was critical.

Around August 15, harvest time would arrive. I was five years old when I first became involved. This was my contribution to paying off the Farm Security loan. The last two weeks of August were the hottest of the year, with temperatures normally ninety-eight degrees or higher. The cornstalks obstructed what little breeze we had. The dried stalks and Johnsongrass cast scratchy debris under our clothes, and we had to be alert for the scorpions that made their home between the outer and inner shuck casings.

These creatures from hell would sometimes travel down our shirts! Their sting was far from lethal, but they always scared me to death.

Harvesting corn involved three workers who pulled corn while walking on each side of and behind a mule-drawn wagon. My job was to prompt the mules forward, advancing them to a distance of twenty-five to thirty feet ahead of the pullers. When the pullers worked their way up to the waiting wagon, it was time for the wagon to move. The row behind the wagon was known as the "down row" because the wagon flattened the cornstalks to a level of about a foot off the ground. Ears were removed from their stalks by placing one hand on the bottom of the ear to act as a fulcrum, and pulling down on the ear with the other hand. Ears were then thrown into the wagon. Every now and then I would get hit in the back by a flying ear of corn. The pullers would have a good laugh. I don't remember if it hurt, but I would never show it. I was in charge of the mules, which in my mind made me the boss. I didn't even object to the musty animal smells that drifted off the sweaty backs of Mike and Tobe. Farming was not for sissies, and I just knew my job was by far the most important. Without me, the mules had to be navigated by one of the pullers on the side of the wagon. This often made it difficult to control the animals' erratic behavior.

At the end of each row, Dad would climb into the wagon, negotiate the turn and send me down the next row. A two-by-ten-inch board lay across the top of the sideboards on the front of the wagon and served as my makeshift seat. Mom made a cushion for me from a flour sack and stuffed it with cotton. Dad nailed the pad onto the board.

Once the wagon was full, we shoveled the corn into the barn through a west-facing window, under the relentless heat of the afternoon sun. Indeed, everything about harvesting corn served to increase our desire to conserve the golden treasure.

From the dried corn we made cornmeal, much as Native Americans and Mexicans had been doing for centuries. First we would shuck the corn and then shell it, using a hand-operated corn sheller. An ear of corn was placed into the sleeve and as the wheel turned, the teeth on the inside wall of the sheller would extract the corn. As demanding as the process was, it sure beat shelling by hand.

After filling three or four 100-pound sacks with shelled corn, we traveled to the mill in Oak Forest, where an electric grinder converted our raw product into meal. Typically, we would leave Oak Forest with enough cornmeal for several months of cornbread. At times, weevils would get into the meal. This was no big deal for us because we put the weevil-infested meal in the slop and fed it to the hogs.

Cornbread, the major product derived from the meal, was the epitome of Depression food: it was cheap. It was a "stick-to-the-ribs" food, containing cornmeal, flour, eggs, hog lard, milk or clabber, ground pork cracklings (optional), salt and baking powder. This was before cholesterol was discovered.

The corn that we stored in the barn was feed for the farm animals. Hogs could tear corn from the cob with their sharp teeth and strong jaws. Chickens and turkeys had no such ability; they had to be fed shelled corn. Cows were even more inept. If we had fed corn on the cob to the cows, they would have swallowed the cob as well as the corn, an unhealthy move even for a 1,000-pound animal. So for cows, we crushed some of our corn—cob, shuck and all—while we were at the mill. In this way we supplied the cows with nutrition from the corn and roughage and filler from the cob and shuck. What a marvelous labor saver—not having to shuck or shell their feed before we crushed it. I was all for that.

The next spring, before the new crop came in, our corncrib had to be cleaned by removing what was left of the past year's supply. By then, about all that could be done with the remaining corn was to crush it for the cows because it usually had become a home for weevils and rats. Cleaning out the crib was an exciting event for Butch and Pudge, our rat terriers. They delighted in catching the scurrying rats as the corn was removed. When a shovel entered the pile of corn, a rat would try to escape by dashing out and climbing up the wall, hoping to exit through the window. The terriers would leap high, grab the escapee and, in a split second, sink their teeth into it, leaving the planet with one less varmint. One year they bagged more than sixty rats. I thought that was even more exciting than coon hunting.

After the 1947 harvest season, we bought our first tractor. It was a brand-new, red-and-gray Ford with a rear-hydraulic lift. Complete with night lights, it had a state-of-the-art system for changing plows. I have to admit that I was happy to see Mike and Tobe retire.

In the fall of 1949, harvesting was done with a mechanical corn puller. This meant no more down rows, no more debris under the collar and no more scorpions. Whoever invented this machine should have received a Nobel Prize. This marvelous invention would churn up and down the rows, two at a time, extracting corn from the stalks. Then, by way of a conveyor belt, the machine would transport the ears into a trailer that followed behind. Mechanical corn pulling was done by contract. A spirited local entrepreneur bought the machine and performed the service for pay. If a farmer couldn't pay with money, he paid with a share of the fresh corn.

Eventually much of the harvesting work became mechanized, but shoveling corn from the trailer to the crib never did. That was a job for Dad and me. Dad was lean, with big, muscular forearms and biceps he had developed over a lifetime of manual labor. Along with his physical strength, he possessed great stamina. I was just starting to build my physical strength. In my junior high and high school days, I knew that football season was approaching, and the harder I worked, the better prepared I would become for two-a-days. Today, some would call our time together "male bonding." In those days, we called it hard work. Both claims are true.

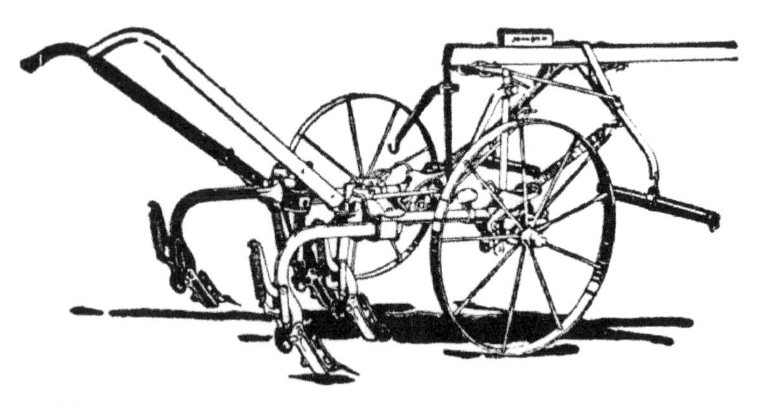

I liked the walking cultivator. I could sweep between the corn and cotton plants by manipulating the handles to knock out cockleburs and Johnsongrass.

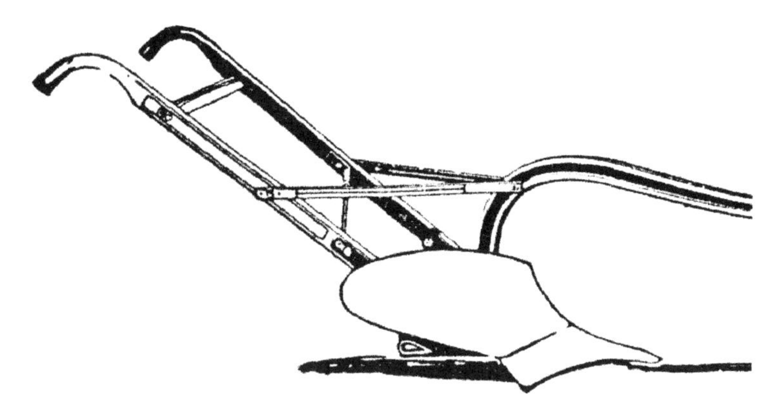

This is the sweep stalk for running the middles in corn. At age 10, I was not ready for prime time. Dad kindly said, "You just need more beans."

My first real job at age five was advancing the wagon, powered by Mike and Tobe, to stay ahead of the corn pullers as they tossed the ears of corn into the wagon.

Popcorn

I never thought I'd hear myself say farming was fun. But it was when it came to growing popcorn. Contrary to modern thinking, popcorn doesn't come from the local movie theater. It's a variety of corn with kernels that contain little soft starch. Heat causes the water in the kernel to expand, and the kernel pops—and you have a real treat. The growing process was an easy project, and anticipating the result was part of the fun.

Popcorn was planted in the spring in the same manner as regular corn, but the mechanism that dropped the seed from the mule-drawn planter was adjusted to accommodate the smaller kernels. It was not necessary to thin the plants because we weren't looking for maximum yield. The harvesting process was also different. When the corn was brown, dry and hanging down from the stalk, we gathered it, which took only a few hours. We shucked it in the field, so we had no cleanup. I don't know why, but popcorn didn't have as much silk as regular corn. One more of those "whys," but who cares. It did make the process a little easier.

We shelled the corn off the cob by hand under the oak tree in the backyard. We shelled by hand because the ears were too small for the mechanical sheller. We put the kernels in fruit jars and coffee cans. The coffee cans were used first because they had no lids. The fruit jars had tight-fitting lids, and that fended off the weevils.

The recipe for truly great popcorn is quite simple. Put a little hog lard in the bottom of a large, two-handle pot along with three or four kernels of corn. When the kernels pop, the grease is hot enough for the major event. Pour in just enough kernels to cover the bottom of the pot. No crowding. Place a tight lid on the pot, watch and wait. Momentarily, the kernels will start exploding. The vessel will tremble and the corn will pop. It's important to shake the pot so every kernel pops, although we all used to fight over the half-pops.

Pour the hot popcorn into a large bowl, return the pot to the stove and add *real* butter. Salt the corn, pour the melted butter on top and let the good times roll. To be quite honest, I think it's the hog lard, the fresh kernels and the real butter that makes this so delicious. Not easy to duplicate that today. (Can you even buy hog lard anymore?)

We didn't have a television, so our "theater" popcorn was consumed as we sat on the front porch, told silly stories and laughed… and laughed.

DAD:
MY HERO

When I reflect on the life of my dad, the one word that comes to mind is "strength." Not necessarily physical strength, although for a man who stood five feet nine inches tall and weighed 150 pounds, he was amazingly strong. Years of farm labor combined with a disciplined mind gave him callused hands, hard shoulders and a back of steel. There was not an ounce of fat on his wiry frame. I was always amazed at his physical stamina. I never once heard him say he was tired.

The word "strength" really applies to my dad's character. Strength of character isn't inherited; it comes from a sense of duty to God, family and community. Dad's German-immigrant parents had little to start with when they arrived in Gonzales around 1895. A baker by trade, Grandpa Schrader had to take up farming to feed his family. And it took his entire family of four boys and two girls working together just to scratch out a living.

Dad was born in a farmhouse on the banks of the Guadalupe River in 1902. The environment into which he was born gave him a fighting chance but little opportunity to succeed. He had little schooling and no career options.

Dad went to school only when his farm duties permitted. As a result, he barely finished the fifth grade. I know he always regretted his lack of education. But he was determined his children would not suffer the same fate. He encouraged us to do well in school, take odd jobs in town and work toward a college education. When he realized that my means to a college education was football, he gladly did my assigned farm chores while I spent afternoons on the practice field.

Dad had learned to farm and he learned well. He was never exposed to any other occupation. In 1922 he began to farm on his own. In 1928 when he married Mom, he continued farming, eventually buying his own farm with the help of a Farm Security loan. He remained a farmer for much of the rest of his life.

Dad taught me how to work. The physical strength, stamina and grit I developed by working side-by-side with him made me a better football player and a better businessman. Dad never forced me to compete; it just happened that way. Living with the pressure to perform was a way of life for him. He was mentally tough, and I wanted to be just like him.

One night when I was about twelve, we were sitting on the front porch and Dad asked, "Buddy, what percentage of the time are you completely honest?" I didn't really know how to answer him. I knew 100 percent was wrong, so I said, "Oh, about 90 percent." I thought that was a good answer. "So," he said, "10 percent of your life you're dishonest." "Wow," I thought. I had no legitimate response after that. But it made me think about how often I did compromise the truth. For Dad, honesty was an absolute. That was a tough act for me to follow, but I always kept the goal in sight as I grew up. I am so grateful to him for his leadership. If I could spend one evening of my life with any person, past or present, I would choose my Dad. I would like to thank him. He was my all-time hero.

Dad had a conservative business philosophy, probably because his own father never seemed to make ends meet.

Dad referred to his nearly destitute childhood a number of times. It made quite an impression on him. He also saw other people being forced into bankruptcy and foreclosure. In one case, according to a friend of Dad's, a neighbor worked hard and finally saved enough for a down payment on a John Deere tractor. That summer the bottom fell out of the cotton market; the price dropped to four cents a pound. The neighbor, unable to meet his tractor payment at the end of the season, could only watch as the tractor was repossessed. He had to go back to farming with mules. The following year, as fate would have it, cotton prices rose to ten cents a pound! But farming with mules is far less productive than farming with a tractor. Instead of reaping a handsome profit, the neighbor scraped by. The woes of a cotton farmer—if it wasn't the weather, it was the fickle market prices.

Dad endured during the hard times. Armed with strong principles and a strong constitution, he steered his family, leading by example. He was too busy tending to his responsibilities to become depressed. Discouraged at times, I'm sure, but letting up or giving up never crossed his mind. Burn out? Dad never knew what that was. His goals were simple and straightforward: protect and care for his family by applying the principles of honesty and hard work. Regardless of how difficult the times were, he never compromised those principles. His loyalty to us created a sense of security that bound our family together. The first thought that came to my mind when I was tempted to get into trouble was how disappointed my dad would be. He had done too much for me to let him down.

Dad had one of the best temperaments of anyone I have ever known. He was kind to his fellow man. When being nice to black people was not a common practice, he treated them with dignity and respect. Dad was proud to have as a friend Lonnie Smith, a good neighbor who happened to be black. Dad often hired Lonnie to help during harvest time but never as a subordinate—always as an equal. Lonnie and Dad would share their lunch under a large tree in the field and exchange stories about their families. Lonnie had an infectious laugh. When I heard them talking together, it warmed my heart.

Dad delegated the discipline of the kids to Mom. He was too kindhearted to be comfortable with that chore. On a few occasions, however, he would lose his patience. When he was the one who administered punishment, I knew I was really in trouble. After our first fall harvest on the home place in 1941, Dad and Uncle Walter were building our barn. They sent me to the house to get some matches so Uncle Walter could have a smoke break. I returned and gave the matches to Uncle Walter. I was intrigued by fire, as most five-year-old boys are, and I ratholed one match. An hour later, I wandered away near a haystack. I made a pile of straw and set it on fire. Quick as a flash, the fire ran up the haystack. I screamed! Uncle Walter and Dad came running. They slung sheets of tin intended for the barn roof against the haystack. That smothered the fire and saved the hay. Dad took me behind the barn, even though it was not finished, and administered corporal punishment. It had been an eventful day. Dad put out one fire, and he put another one on my backside. My "pyro" days were over.

Typically, Dad got up before dawn, milked the cows, and worked in the field until mid-day. After the midday meal, he would take a half-hour nap before returning to work. He quit at dark and was often in bed by 9:00 p.m. He took off on Saturday afternoon so we could do our weekly shopping and socializing in town. He never worked on Sunday. His work and family responsibilities left little time for himself, so he really never had a hobby. The little spare time he had revolved around church, visiting with friends and relatives, and playing dominoes.

Dad was an excellent domino player. He would frequent the domino hall on the town square on Saturday afternoon and sometimes played with friends at their homes. The game that the men played was straight dominoes. After each shuffle, the players took seven "rocks" each. Each player would play a domino in turn, until they finished the "hand." Usually, after the second or third play, Dad knew what everyone had in his hand. When I was his opponent, after his third lead, he would say, "I'll take that trey-deuce" (or whatever). I would think: "How did you know I had the trey-deuce?" He had the experience and concentration to play the game well.

Dad had a good sense of humor and a dry wit. He often said, "When it gets hopeless, all we can hope for is it doesn't get any worse." When things did get really tough, Dad demonstrated strong leadership. Early one morning in the spring of 1942, I woke to hear Mom crying. Dad and Mom were standing on the front porch, looking down at the San Marcos River valley where the flood waters had covered our young crops. I looked at Dad; he stood there like a statue, clenching his teeth, looking straight ahead, saying nothing. At that time, I couldn't tell what his demeanor meant. But now I know. It meant determination. He was saying: "We are going to make it because we have the strength and courage to fight on." In the midst of a crisis, he made us feel better and he gave us hope. The flood that year did do some damage, but the water receded quickly and we ended up having a fair year.

Dad lived a long life and had a peaceful passing at age eighty-three. Fortunately, he did not have to fight death. He had fought enough battles during the Depression. The Depression made him stronger, and he made me a better man. Charlie Schrader was a man of great character. He was a good man.

Food:
A Recipe for Happiness

Many people who lived through the Depression have said, "We were poor, but we didn't know it." That always perplexed me; it seemed pretty obvious that we were poor. I finally came to realize that the main criterion for the poverty line was food supply. If you were ever really hungry, you were poor. By this standard, we were blessed.

We always had enough to eat, though never an overabundance (except at a social or church event). I never missed a meal, and everyone in our family had a healthy appetite. We always ate everything Mom prepared, leaving little for the hogs or family dogs. Yet no one was fat. Our meals were delicious, nutritious and prepared with pride.

Occasionally we had to make room for others at the table. During busy harvest times when Dad hired a few field hands, the midday meal was part of their pay. And if one of Mom's sewing customers showed up for a fitting and the visiting got interesting, she would invite the customer (and her husband and kids) to stay for supper. We always seemed to have enough food for unexpected company.

Mom cooked on a wood-burning cookstove for the first fifteen years of her homemaking career. She and Dad had bought the stove second-hand soon after they were married in 1928. It was a simple, straightforward, no-maintenance appliance that would perform forever.

The stove consisted of an oven, six burners (eyes), two warming boxes and a firebox. The firebox was located on the left side. On the floor of the firebox was an iron grate that controlled air circulation. Heated air circulated around the oven and under the burners. Stove-top temperatures were adjusted by moving the pots from one burner to another. The temperature of a burner depended upon its location and size and on whether its cover was removed. Oven temperatures were adjusted by moving the baking item to a different rack level, opening the oven door if it got too hot, adding more wood to the fire if the temperature dropped too low, or adjusting the damper on the stovepipe. Ash and soot trays had to be emptied often.

The firebox required a specific size of wood. Dad, Brother and I chopped the wood and kept the wood box on the back porch full. In the winter, Dad would make a fire in the potbelly stove in the living room early in the morning. This began to heat the house. After milking the cows, he would return and transfer hot coals to the cook-stove firebox, using a shovel and metal bucket. By then, Mom was up and ready to cook breakfast. On warm mornings, he started the fire directly in the cookstove.

Mom cooked on her stove three times a day, seven days a week. The labor-intensive system never seemed to deter Mom's program. Her mission was to provide us with the most nutritious, best-tasting food with lots of variety. Often she would cook a pot of pinto beans and leave it on the stove all day. (Why the beans didn't spoil, I'll never know.) That was our ace-in-the-hole food. If I was passing by the stove and I was hungry, I would slice a piece of bread and make a cold bean sandwich. That was a real stick-to-the-ribs snack.

Four or five times a week, Mom made loaf bread, dinner rolls and cornbread. I will never forget walking over the hill after the school bus dropped me off and smelling Mom's bread as it was cooking. (Only a mother would have such good timing.) Three or four slices (a half loaf) with fresh butter and jam would tide me over until supper.

Mom cooked cornbread in a round pie pan and sliced it into six equal pieces. When Brother was a growing teenager, he would get the sixth slice—no dividing. I often thought how nice it would be when he went off to college. I would get his slice and the extra one, too.

Biscuits were often served for breakfast, and oatmeal cookies were a regular treat. Pies and cobblers were usually limited to Sundays and special events, except in the spring when dewberries were in abundance. Cakes were a rarity because of the difficulty of controlling oven temperature.

In 1943 my parents replaced the wood stove with a kerosene cookstove, a tremendous upgrade. Kerosene had its limitations, however, because of the fire hazard and the limit on temperature capabilities. Two years later we got a butane-gas cookstove (and a living room heater), which moved our quality of life a giant step forward.

Another essential kitchen component was the icebox. It was more like a piece of cabinetry than a refrigerator—low on performance and high on maintenance. It had one compartment for a block of ice and other compartments for storing perishable food. Because the ice would melt, the icebox required frequent and thorough cleaning to combat the resulting mold and slime. The environment was perfect for bacterial growth. Emptying the drip pan was a routine chore.

During most of the year the temperature in the icebox was not adequate to preserve food, only to delay its spoilage. The temperature of milk would be slightly lower than room temperature. Sometimes in the summer, we would add a little ice to glasses of milk, but that was a rare treat because ice was saved for tea.

Butter would not keep in the icebox in the summer, so we had to store it in the well. We always had plenty of butter and used the extra as barter to help pay for other supplies. Just before departing for town, we retrieved the bricks of butter and immediately upon arriving in town, we dropped them off at the grocery store before they turned into shapeless globs.

Ice lasted about three or four days in the cooler months but only two days in the summer. That meant Mom had to achieve a delicate balance: harvesting from the garden only what she could preserve and what we could quickly eat. It was an art as well as a science.

Most of our food came from the farm. The foodstuffs we had to buy were staples like flour, sugar and salt. During World War II, sugar was rationed; that was a real sacrifice because we consumed quite a bit. Mom controlled the sugar bowl. Iced tea was served pre-sweetened.

Among our food purchases was a small amount of beef. We always had a few head of cattle, but we raised them to sell their calves. We didn't have the resources to butcher a cow and preserve the beef. On Saturday night, after shopping in town, our meal was special: pan-fried steak. It was an inexpensive cut of beef—but a treat for us, nevertheless.

Our Sunday dinner (the midday meal) was usually pot roast and vegetables. Combining potatoes, carrots and onions with the roast simplified the cooking process and added great flavor to the vegetables. Experience taught Mom exactly how much fire would cook the pot roast for the two and a half hours that we were in Sunday school and church. Sunday supper usually consisted of leftovers (if there were any) from the large noon meal. The back-up meal was bacon and eggs.

Pork was the most popular meat for our family, and we had plenty of it. Our hog butchering provided us with bacon, ham, chops and sausage.

Next to pork, we ate lots of chicken. Fryers were economical to produce, and they grew fast. Chicken posed no preservation issue because we ate an entire fryer in one sitting.

In the early years, we bought baby chicks from a mail-order house. We received a notice in the mail that the chicks were at the post office waiting to be picked up. It was a miracle that they survived the rigors of travel and the time required to finally reach Gonzales. Remarkably, the mortality rate was low; we lost only about three or four from an order of twenty-five. Later we used a local source for chicks: Boothe Hatchery in Gonzales.

It took about five weeks for a chick to grow large enough to eat. This gave us a constant supply of four or five chickens a week. We never got tired of Mom's fried chicken and the delicious gravy made from the drippings left in the skillet. Chicken and dumplings were another treat. When the last three or four chickens had grown beyond the premium size for frying, Mom baked them with cornbread dressing. I still miss the taste of "fresh" chicken.

A chick's diet was corn and maize (produced on the farm) and chicken feed that we bought at the feed store. When we added the cost of feed to the price of a baby chick (ten cents each), a fryer ready for consumption cost approximately thirty cents. It's easy to understand why this was a popular Depression dish.

To cook chicken for dinner or supper, Mom put a pot of water on the stove to boil while Brother or I captured the chicken. We used a stiff wire about six feet long with a hook on one end to hook the chicken's leg just above the claw. We grabbed the chicken and took it to a tree stump next to the chicken house. We held the victim down and gave it one quick whack on the neck with an ax. A reflex action in the bird caused it to jump and twist around for a few minutes, even without a head!

Once when Sis had a girlfriend (a city girl) over to visit, I asked if she wanted to watch some fun. She had no idea what she was about to see. When the ax came down, she screamed. She continued screaming as the chicken jerked and writhed in its spasm of death. Mom, hearing the scream, rushed out of the house, thinking something terrible had happened. She saw the headless chicken twitching and me laughing. Then she scolded me for scaring our guest.

After chopping off the chicken's head, we dipped it into a pot of boiling water for a few seconds to condition the skin for easy feather removal. Mom cut the chicken open and dumped the innards and other inedible parts into the slop bucket. Then she cut up the fryer, dusted the parts with flour, salt and pepper and placed them in a skillet of cold lard. From the chicken yard to the kitchen table took about twenty-five minutes. It was an efficient operation.

In addition to providing meat, chickens produced eggs. Eggs were another "stick-to-the-ribs" Depression food. High in protein, they were a quick and nutritious meal in themselves as well as an indispensable ingredient in many dishes. Eggs, along with bacon and ham, were our most frequent breakfast meal. When the price of eggs rose dramatically during World War II, we sold them by the dozens—a welcome contribution to the farm's cash flow.

Another chicken contribution was fertilizer. Chicken manure becomes fertilizer when it dries out completely, eliminating the offensive odor and other undesirable aspects of fresh manure. Chicken fertilizer was used in the garden, on the lawn and on yard shrubs. Dad once made the mistake of spreading the lawn with manure that had not dehydrated sufficiently. It produced a rank odor that flowed through the open windows of the house. Dad, with his busy schedule, was trying to accommodate Mom's wishes for a beautiful yard. From then on, he was careful to cover the lawn with chicken fertilizer, not chicken manure.

Our milk cows provided us with fresh whole milk, butter and cheese. Dad, Brother and I would drink more than a gallon and a half of milk a day. Milk also supplemented the diet of our dogs, cats and hogs. We always had two cows in production. Both were mixed-breed animals with some Jersey and some Holstein blood that made them good producers. Dad milked them both early in the morning and again in the early evening when he finished working in the field. The two cows would produce about five gallons a day. A pure-bred dairy cow with a proper diet could produce up to six gallons a day.

After milking, Dad would set the milk in the icebox to let the cream rise to the top. Later the cream was scooped up and put into the butter churn. The kids usually churned the cream after supper with a hand crank that turned a paddle and propelled the cream in motion. (This churn was an upgrade from Grandma's crock-and-plunger system.) Within a short time, yellow specks of butter began to appear in the churn's glass bowl. Gradually the bits of butter collected into globs, leaving behind a white, watery liquid. Mom spooned the butter out of the bowl and pressed it into a rectangular wooden mold. (The remaining liquid was thrown out to the hogs.) She used butter in many vegetable and dessert dishes, and we bartered three or four pounds of butter at the grocery store every week.

During the early and mid-forties, we produced thirty dozen eggs and four pounds of butter a week. That covered the cost of our groceries, a twenty-five pound block of ice and an occasional dollar's worth of gas for Blackie.

Cheese was made by putting clumps of clabber (curdled sour milk) into a cheesecloth and hanging it on a fence or tree limb. The whey (the watery part) would drain through the cloth onto the ground, and heat would turn the remaining clabber into a kind of crumbly cottage cheese.

We had two gardens: one in the spring and another in the fall. In the spring garden, we planted more than a dozen vegetables including potatoes, tomatoes, sweet corn, green beans and blackeyed peas. In the fall garden, we grew cabbage, cauliflower, broccoli and leaf lettuce.

Potatoes were a perfect Depression food and were on our table almost every day. The cost of production was almost zero. All it took was a lot of time and effort. The plants for next year's crop came from the current year's harvest. As spring approached, white sprouts would emerge from the potatoes' eyes. We would cut up each potato into five or six chunks, each chunk supporting at least one sprout, and plant these sprouts in a prepared bed. Within a few days, each sprout would shoot up through the dirt as a leafy, green potato plant.

In late spring we dug up the potato plants and harvested the tubers clinging to the roots. We stored the potatoes under the house, which was the coolest, driest area available. By late winter of the next year, we had almost exhausted the inventory. We took the remainder of the supply and put them in a warmer environment so they could produce sprouts for spring planting.

Mashed potatoes, made with fresh milk and butter, was our favorite dish, especially when Mom served it with fried-chicken gravy. We enjoyed many potato dishes, including boiled and buttered red potatoes and mashed and baked yams, also from our garden.

Onions were a big item from the garden, essential for seasoning meats, vegetables and salads. Like potatoes, the onions were stored under the house. We hung bunches of them with strings attached to nails in the floor beams.

Tomatoes were produced twice a year: spring and fall. During peak harvest time in the spring, Mom served tomatoes three meals a day.

Many garden vegetables, including sweet corn, green beans and blackeyed peas, were canned. The number of canned items and jars of food that we "put up" was determined by the number of cans and jars we could afford. Cans were cheaper, but jars were recyclable.

Canning was labor-intensive. Mom did most of the actual canning, but much of the preparation was done with child labor (Brother, Sis and me). We had to snap the beans, shell the peas and shuck the corn. The unspoken rule was, "If you're going to consume it, you're going to contribute to its production." It was a frequent and subtle reminder that we were each required to pull our load.

The entire family worked in the garden every Saturday morning. During the harvest period we consumed as much as possible, canned as much as possible, and gave away the rest to friends, neighbors, kinfolks and the preacher.

One of the most common Depression foods was corn. We ate cornbread, cornbread dressing, cornmeal mush, cornmeal cakes, corn fritters and hush puppies. We ate corn roasted on the cob, skillet-fried with chopped bacon, and cream-style with milk, butter and sugar.

We had many tasty treats from the wild. In the spring, we gathered dewberries (first cousins to blackberries) to use in pies and cobbler. The thick and thorny vines made harvesting difficult. That was a minor inconvenience, however, compared to the real threat—copperheads! Once when Dad and I were picking berries, we spotted a copperhead and moved out of its range. We continued picking until Dad sighted a second viper. "Let's get out of here Buddy!" he shouted. "Dewberry cobbler is good but not good enough to hang around here."

A wild pear tree provided fruit for pear preserves. Wild grapes were made into jelly and wine. (The wine was exclusively Grandpa Vackar's project, and I was his assistant.) Occasionally Uncle Walter gave us honey from his beehives. In the fall we gathered pecans from the native trees in the river bottom for pecan pie (made with ribbon cane molasses).

When we first moved to the home place, we would catch catfish on throw lines in the San Marcos River. Fresh catfish rolled in cornmeal and fried in lard was terrific. Tragically, in 1944, an oil company upstream dumped chemical waste into the river and caused a massive fish kill. Seeing the dead fish floating down the river was a distressing sight. I heard the company was never punished. That ended a tasty food source and a major source of pleasure.

Every now and then we would kill a few squirrels in the river bottom. After they were skinned and cleaned, they looked like rats. I never cared for squirrels for that reason. Sis would never eat them.

Although our family heritage was German and Czech, ethnic foods did not play a significant role in our normal fare. Our food choices were dictated by what we could produce and preserve. However, one Czech pastry, kolaches, was popular at Mom's family reunions. Prune and poppy-seed filling were the two most requested varieties.

When Dad got hungry, he would simply sit down at the kitchen table. Mom didn't have to look at the clock; she knew it was time to fix dinner (or supper).

Breakfast was a wonderful meal. Mom prepared many scrumptious items from the following list: bacon, ham, sausage, eggs, fritters, biscuits, pancakes, oatmeal, sliced tomatoes (in season) and pinto beans. The greatest of all were fritters. A fritter is a thin pancake, much like a crepe. Mom cooked fritters in iron skillets with a little bacon grease or lard to avoid sticking. She would have two skillets going at once to keep up with the demand. We put fresh butter and ribbon cane molasses or wild grape jelly on top, and then rolled the fritter up like a crepe. It's embarrassing to think now how many fritters Brother and

I could consume at one sitting. Dad would delight in watching the show, while Mom hardly had time to look up. Sis may have had one or two.

At the time none of us knew about cholesterol or thought about "carbs." Much of our diet would be blacklisted today. Physical activity and the absence of junk food may partially explain why we were so healthy.

Only bare necessities like plates and forks were put on the table. There were no napkins—cloth or paper. Cloth napkins were out of the question because laundering was too laborious. Paper was not an option; it was a luxury we could not afford. Dad kept a cup towel in his lap. It was passed around upon request. At the conclusion of a meal, if your teeth needed to be picked, you used a broom straw.

Mom's good sense of smell kept the atmosphere pleasant. Working in and around the barnyard meant that residue from the animal droppings often ended up on our shoes. (In my case, the residue stuck to the bottom of my bare feet. The soles of my feet were so thick, I could have had a build-up of foreign substances and never known it.) As we took our places at the table, Mom would say, "OK, someone needs to check their soles." Everyone who had been exposed would go outside and remove their shoes (or wash their feet).

After we settled into our chairs, we said a brief prayer in unison. It was essential to thank the Lord for our many blessings and ask him to forgive our sins. The next ten minutes or so were usually spent in silence as we passed around the food and filled our plates. Conversation during the meal was brief—we were always hungry and wanted to be first for seconds, in case there were any.

At the end of the meal, Dad would begin the conversation by talking about the events of the day and what needed to be accomplished in the days ahead. Back then, "children were seen and not heard," so the kids often spoke only in answer to a question. We did plenty of listening. After Sis and I were excused from the table, Brother would remain to talk with Dad about "adult" issues. I never knew exactly what those issues were. Sis and I took care of the dishes; she washed and I dried.

Mealtime was a significant family event. It fed the body, nourished the spirit, focused on important family and world events and reaffirmed that we were all partners in life.

Mom's Fresh Fried Chicken

1 1½-pound chicken from the chicken yard
1 large pot of boiling water
ample hog lard
flour
salt and pepper

Catch and behead chicken. Dip bird into hot water and pluck feathers. Dress chicken by removing entrails and feet. Cut into family-size portions and roll in flour, salt and pepper.

Place a generous amount of hog lard into a large skillet. Add chicken to pan while grease is still cold. Cook until all pieces are crisp and brown. Turn once.

Serves 5

Preparation and cooking time: 25 minutes

Cream Gravy

Drain off most of the hot grease, leaving some grease and drippings in the skillet. Add flour (not too much) and salt and pepper. Cook rapidly (not too fast) stirring constantly until brown. Slowly add milk or water, and stir until gravy is smooth.

Roastin' Ears Supreme

1 pot of boiling water
fresh ears of corn
salt and pepper
butter

Place large pot of water on the stove to boil.* Send kids to the field to select young, tender ears of corn. Shuck and silk corn ears, and place in boiling water for 8 minutes. Remove ears, cover with butter, salt and pepper, and enjoy.

Preparation and cooking time: 20 minutes

*Correct procedure is essential for maximum freshness. The water should begin to heat before the corn is gathered.

Mom never had a cookbook. She always seemed to know what to do and just how to do it with whatever ingredients she had on hand. I assume she learned all her cooking skills as a young girl. I took all that for granted, but I now greatly appreciate her skill and talent.

Ribbon Cane Molasses

Fortunately for me, the farm provided a homemade remedy for my sweet tooth: ribbon cane molasses. Mom would smother her homemade fritters with the sweet, dark syrup. I used to think I had never tasted anything so good. We all felt privileged to enjoy such a special treat during hard economic times.

Dad and I planted the ribbon cane seeds, which we bought for twenty-five cents at Dawe's Feed & Seed, in the patch down by the windmill in late March. The stalks grew fast. By late June we were ready to gather the crop and reap the rewards of the harvest. It was just too tempting for me not to sample the new crop a little early. Chewing on a tender, juicy stalk while I fished in the creek made for a pretty cool afternoon.

One year we tried sorghum cane, but that proved to be a mistake. Sorghum syrup was too bitter and robust for our taste. "Maybe they like this in East Texas," Dad said, "but we like our molasses smoother." Regardless of the taste, we endured the sorghum to the last drop. It was better than nothing, and nothing was not an option. Grandpa Vackar was the only person who liked sorghum, so he got lucky. We were generous with our giveaway that year.

The cane harvesting process was basic: we cut each stalk with a knife, stripped the leaves by hand and left them on the ground to be plowed under at a later date. The cane was not allowed to touch the ground—dirt could never mix with the cane juice. The naked stalks were placed in the wagon for transport to the mill. The stalks were stacked high and firmly tied down. I liked to ride on top of the precarious load. I discovered just how precarious it was when we hit a chuckhole and I slid off onto the ground. It was a big fall, but I made a soft landing: I hit feet first with no injury. (I was lucky. Cactus grew profusely in the road, and there was little traffic to trample its growth.) Falling off was really kind of fun, like sliding down a slide.

The mill belonged to a neighbor about a mile down the road. The only fee for the use of the mill was two small buckets of molasses. Both Tobe and Mike pulled the old wagon up to the mill. When we arrived, we unhitched Tobe so he could power the press. My job was critical: I would follow the mule in a circle, making sure he kept moving—whether he liked it or not. Tobe responded positively to my tapping his rump with the reins—I felt quite important at the ripe old age of six.

We took the cane from the wagon and fed it into the press. The press consisted of a large, heavy, metal wheel that rolled over an elevated, concrete bowl. The bowl was slightly tapered to the middle with a hole in the center. Under the hole, a tub caught the juice as it was squeezed from the cane. Nothing high-tech, just simple gravity flow. We removed the spent stalks from the press and threw them on the ground. Dad and our neighbor performed the main function at the press.

We removed the tub from the press and poured the syrup into a wash pot that was already sitting on a roaring fire. The cooking process began. We frequently stirred the syrup with a wooden paddle, continually monitoring and tasting the sweet juice. When the taste and texture were perfect, we removed the pot from the fire. Texture was extremely important. It took experience and skill to know when the molasses had cooked long enough to maintain perfect consistency for a smooth flow. Dad had a knack for knowing exactly when that time was. If the syrup was too thick, it would pour too slowly—hence the term, "slow as molasses."

After the syrup cooled, we poured the finished product into two five-gallon milk cans. Lids were secured for the ride home. The cans were tied in the wagon and strapped to the sideboards. If a full can of molasses had ever turned over, it would have been a tragedy. Thank God it never did. I imagine that I would have cried all the way home and that Dad would have locked his jaw and looked straight ahead, not saying a word.

Upon returning home, we stored the fruits of our labor in the kitchen pantry. The cane usually produced about ten gallons—that was enough molasses to last at least until Christmas.

Good homemade molasses tasted wonderful, and we never tired of it. Often it was the only sweet in the house. It was especially popular for breakfast when we ate biscuits, pancakes and fritters. A syrup pitcher was a permanent fixture on our kitchen table along with the salt-and-pepper shakers. When we didn't have a dessert, which was often, a good substitute was molasses and bread or cornbread.

The advent of the tractor and modern technology brought an end to our homemade molasses program. After the war, when sugar rations were lifted, we never resumed the project. We were able to buy syrup at the store and have the luxury of variety. Brer Rabbit was my favorite, but somehow it never tasted quite the same.

MOM:
A REAL PIONEER WOMAN

Of all the stories Grandma Vackar told about the family, my favorite is the account of Mom's first day at school.

It was September of 1914, Grandma would tell, and Gladys sat nervously at her desk in the one-room country school. She had more than the first-day-of-school butterflies—and for good reason: she spoke no English. The family lived in a rural community where Czech was spoken daily and there was no reason to communicate in English, until now. Gladys was the oldest of four, the first to attend school, and she was starting her education with a major handicap. Additionally, girls weren't expected to do well in school. But Gladys listened and learned. It would be only a few months before she was speaking creditable English and teaching it to her parents. It wasn't a major obstacle for this bright, determined five-year-old; it was the beginning of a life motivated by resolve and purpose. A life that touched so many, a life that made this world a better place.

School was important to Mom. The country school at Oak Forest didn't offer the last two years of high school. So at age sixteen, she moved to town. She lived in a boarding house and supported herself by working in the kitchen washing dishes and cooking while she finished high school. Her childhood seemed harsh to me, but she never complained about the way she was raised. She met her responsibilities with little thought of herself. That was her attitude throughout her life, a life she often referred to as blessed.

One of my earliest recollections of Mom goes back to a bitterly cold January morning when I was about five years old. I was wakened by a loud thud, so I followed the sound into the dark living room. Dad had tripped, scattering his load of firewood all over the room. As I watched him collect the wood for our two stoves, I caught sight of Mom in the kitchen. She was scrambling eggs by the light of a kerosene lamp. It was so cold she had a small, homemade quilt wrapped around her shoulders. I shivered and wondered why she didn't wait until daylight to cook breakfast. But daylight marked the time Dad left for the field and Brother and Sis left to catch the school bus. The family had to start every morning with a hearty, healthy breakfast: "Fuel for your engine," Mom would say.

I like to think of Mom as one of the last real pioneer women. She cooked everything from scratch, washed clothes by hand, nursed her babies, made quilts from fabric scraps, and grew vegetables in the garden. She was a tireless worker who never grumbled. She endured the harsh challenges of the Depression and gave selflessly to her family and the community.

When Mom married Dad, women in rural communities were beginning to organize in clubs to learn canning and other skills that could improve the lives of their families and communities. The clubs were led by the Texas A&M University Extension Service and, until the late 1970s, were called Home Demonstration Clubs. Mom was a member of the Gonzales group for fifty-seven years. She lived by their creed, although she could have easily written it herself.

Creed of the Texas Extension Homemakers Association:

> We believe in the sanctity of the home.
>
> We believe the home is the place where love, faith, trust and devotion must be lived each day; where obedience and reverence grow and where God is known.
>
> We believe those within its walls should be taught to work, to play and to have compassion for those less fortunate.
>
> We believe sharing responsibilities is necessary, and that from the fireside will come the citizens who will uphold the best way of life.

While devoted to the demanding work of caring for her family, Mom still found time to be active in social, civic and church organizations. She taught Sunday school at church and Bible school on Saturdays at the Gonzales Warm Springs Foundation for Crippled Children. She did not have time for physical illness, emotional stress, foul moods or depression. She was a selfless, natural giver. Sacrifice was part of her character. She gave to the deserving but she also had a keen ability to recognize the undeserving. She was there when someone needed love, comfort and reinforcement. She knew what to say and how long to stay. She never expected or needed recognition for her kindness and charity, but she accepted compliments with grace and humility.

Mom had an innate sense of class. Many country people did not. I really believe she had the confidence to be comfortable dining with Queen Elizabeth if she ever had the opportunity. She had a presence about her that put everyone else at ease.

Mom equated personal appearance with manners. "If you look your best," she would say, "you will act your best. Manners are priceless, yet they cost nothing." She felt manners were a direct reflection of a person's upbringing, and she made sure her children's appearance and behavior reflected the highest standards.

Mom taught us to look a problem in the eye and deal head-on with adversity. When I was eight or nine years old, several older neighbor children began to taunt me and tried to start a fight. Intimidated, I ran home to ask Mom what to do. She didn't tell me I should stay and fight. She simply said I had to settle it without backing away. I immediately headed back to the neighbors' house. As I looked back, I saw Mom watching me walking down the trail. I knew what I had to do, and Mom knew I was going to preserve my dignity. I arrived back on the scene where my rival and his buddies were eager for some action. Sis was there as my moral support, and Mom was waiting at home. I accepted the dare, walked up to my opponent and gave him a brisk shove. We grabbed one another, hit the ground, rolled around in the dirt about four times and then realized we had had enough. The spectators ruled it a draw, and Mom was proud that I had stood my ground.

Once I went to Mom upset because one of the neighbor kids accused me of stealing. According to the kids, their mother had made the accusation. I told Mom I did nothing wrong: "I didn't steal anything." Mom immediately rose from her sewing machine and proceeded across the pasture to meet with our neighbor. A short time later, Mom returned home with a simple report: "Buddy, she no longer thinks you stole anything!" I can only surmise how the confrontation went. Mom faced the problem with confidence because she knew I was being truthful. She could read me (and everyone else) like a book. I later heard she diplomatically told the neighbor that she had committed a serious offense by falsely accusing me. Mom gracefully accepted the neighbor's apology, gave her a hug and continued their friendship. She let her mind and her heart lead the way.

Mom's sewing business was an amazingly successful enterprise. The first three or four years, Mom had a foot-pedal Singer machine. She later got an electric sewing machine, but the updated model didn't increase production much. She could pedal faster than the electric machine could operate.

She sold an exceptional product for a reasonable price—actually a ridiculously low price. I suppose she would have justified that price by the fact that customers had to endure some inconveniences: we lived five miles out in the country and we had no telephone. But, as a perk, they got to visit with Gladys and occasionally Dad. And because most of the business was transacted in the early evenings, many customers stayed for supper. Fortunately, the preparation of chicken from the yard to the dining room table took only twenty-five minutes.

Mom's price structure was unusual. Full price was reasonable, but few customers ever paid it. Price was based on ability to pay, and that was Mom's call. I remember one family that received a volume discount. They had nine daughters and Mom charged them $1.50 per dress. When the family filed into St. James Catholic Church on Sunday morning, they made quite a statement. Many of those dresses stood the test of time and were passed down three or four times.

Once, after seeing that the sewing orders were increasing, Dad suggested Mom raise her prices. "I can't do that," she said. "These are my friends." Mom never could tell her friends she couldn't take on more business, and everyone was willing to wait when her work piled up.

For years Mom made uniforms for the Apache cheerleaders and majorettes. Sis, a cheerleader, always got to model the latest style. The girls adored Mom when they were kids and valued her friendship when they became adults. During prom season, it was standing room only at our house as the pretty co-eds lined up to be fitted for their gowns. (I was always on hand in case Mom needed my help.) Often Mom designed the dresses, making her own patterns customized for each girl. Cousin Lynda still remarks about Mom's talent: "Once I designed a contest twirling uniform, and Aunt Gladys made it from my measurements (perfect fit). I was so proud."

Mom's mission when she started the business was to make money for "extras" for us. Like many other facets of her life, her heart led the way in her sewing business, and pleasure and success followed.

Mom personified the joy of giving. Shortly after January 1 every year, she would begin producing gifts for the following Christmas. These special gifts were made from her hands and came from her heart. Our scarcity of money didn't present a problem for Mom—it gave her an opportunity to be creative and to give with the labor of love.

She sewed for her customers during the day and worked on her handmade presents in the evening. When I was ten, I opened a Christmas gift Mom made especially for me. I couldn't believe my eyes! It was a black cowboy shirt with snaps on the front and sleeves, with stitched arrowheads on the corners of both pockets. Across the upper shoulders was a rolling seam line just like the shirts worn by rodeo cowboys. I thought it looked just like those shirts worn by my favorite western-movie hero, Lash LaRue. My hand-me-down black boots with decorative stars were two sizes too small, but they didn't hurt my feet that Christmas morning. The shirt made me feel as though I were a real cowboy.

Every year, after the Christmas tree was trimmed, neatly wrapped gifts began to appear underneath it. They gave our home a wonderful spirit of Christmas and reinforced to the family what giving really meant. I'm sure Mom gave no thought to the work, and we were not fully conscious of just how much effort she put into it. One Christmas I counted twenty-six handmade gifts. Every year she said, "I wish I had more time because there are always people I leave out." Among the prized gifts she made were afghans, doilies, quilts, tissue-box holders, dolls with Mom-made clothes, decorative pot holders, recipe holders, baby blankets, booties and numerous crocheted items. Christmas was a perfect season for Mom—and she was perfect for the Christmas season.

Mom had an unending devotion to Dad. Once (and only once) when I criticized Dad, Mom gave me a tongue-lashing: "Compare what you do for your Dad with what he does for you. Where do you think you would be if your Dad didn't dedicate his life to your welfare? Can you ever repay him? Do you know any father more dedicated to his family?" After that, Mom rose from her sewing machine and began preparing supper. I went outside and spent some needed time with my dog, Pudge.

Mom died in 1997. I think about her every day. Sometimes I wonder what her life would have been like had she been raised in a different era—like the '80s—a time that encouraged women to succeed. She most definitely would have received her college degree and gone on to run her own business. Mom would have been a great CEO: driven, firm, creative and compassionate. She was indeed a special lady.

Cousin Kathy agrees:

"My Aunt Gladys"

by Kathy Vackar

How can just *one* memory or *one* story come to my mind whenever I think of my Aunt Gladys, when she was always larger than life itself! She was always there for everyone and everything, always in a great mood. She always seemed to be in control, so much so that if the word "stress" were even in her vocabulary, it never seemed to be put to use.

Mostly I remember the stability she seemed to provide—not only to her family but also to all those who knew her. She was dependable and all knew they could count on Gladys once she had committed to do something. She was the backbone of many organizations in Gonzales and the "queen of volunteering," not seeking any rewards, way before it was in vogue. She was definitely in the forefront of almost everything she did.

She was talented and creative, providing many citizens of the area with custom-created clothing for so many years. In today's world perhaps she would be the manufacturer of her own line of clothing. She was capable of achieving anything she wanted with those talents she possessed and successfully used to the fullest.

She was there for support, not only for her immediate family but also her friends, church members and anyone that had the privilege of knowing Gladys.

She always put her family first: she provided a clean home, delicious meals on the table and a fun place to come for family gatherings, holidays or just an evening of conversation. She was genuinely interested in all those around her.

Just a couple of weeks ago, as I was browsing a local garden shop and planning the summer landscape for my back patio, the beautiful and colorful zinnias instantly brought the vivid memory of Aunt Gladys and her home to my mind. I could not help but smile as I remembered all the colorful zinnias she always planted along her front fence each summer. I could almost taste the cold and delicious homemade ice cream we would enjoy there in the summer evenings, as we cousins chased the lightning bugs. Remembering that, I came home from the garden shop with several containers of colorful, blooming zinnias that are now sitting on my back patio. And I trust they will make me smile all summer long.

One of my favorite recollections of Aunt Gladys is how well she dressed, especially in her later years. She was always so neat and fashionable, with just the right accessories. Today I consider that a mark of someone who is self-assured, one who enjoys life to the fullest, and enjoys smiling and sharing their joy with others. That indeed was my Aunt Gladys.

Looking back, I like to think of her as the "Rose Kennedy" of her family. Of all the children of Laddie and Julia Vackar, she gave all of us ideals that we have realized are still so important today. I hope there is a part of my Aunt Gladys inside me. If so, then I know I'm on the right path, doing what I'm supposed to be doing, sharing along the way, smiling and enjoying as I continue day to day.

I know for certain each time my Aunt Gladys comes to my mind, a smile comes to my face and a warm and fuzzy feeling rises deep inside me. I just hope I am as fortunate to have someone say that of me once my book of life has been closed. But then again, as I write this remembrance, it's obvious her book of life is *not* closed but still wide open! She is just into deeper chapters, still bringing joy, touching the lives of all those she loved—just as she did to me at the landscape center a couple of weeks ago.

The boarding house across the street from the high school on St. Lawrence Street. Mom lived and worked in the kitchen while she finished high school.

The First Evangelical Lutheran Church

The Schraders were members of the First Evangelical Lutheran Church in Gonzales. Our church, like others in the area, was a mecca for people ravaged by the Depression. It compelled them to rally around one another in the belief that God would take care of them. The church provided a system for the fortunate to help the less fortunate, whether it be in death or in crop failure. One year our Ladies Aid Society, a small group, made twenty-five quilts for needy families in the community. That effort benefited a lot of families, considering that many households had three or four people sleeping under one quilt.

Acts of compassion and kindness were expressions of spiritual and moral principles that we were taught every Sunday. For guidance and direction in these principles, church members looked to the church pastor.

The first pastor I remember was the Reverend Walter Wolff. According to the church history, he was called to Gonzales in 1931 after the congregation went without a pastor for eight months. Times were tough, and the congregation was so small that the church couldn't afford to have its own building. Services were conducted at the North Avenue Ward School. Reverend Wolff was offered a deal he couldn't refuse. In addition to his duties in

Gonzales, he would travel twice a month to Monthalia, fourteen miles west of Gonzales, and lead services at the Lutheran Church there. His salary: three hundred dollars a year, or twelve dollars a service. Car expenses for commuting were not included. It can safely be said he was not in it for the money. There is no record of the compensation package from the Gonzales congregation. Perhaps the deacons were too embarrassed to document the terms of the agreement.

In 1935 a parsonage was built for the Reverend and his family, mostly by volunteer labor. The small house, which was often used for organizational meetings, was a blessing for the seven-member family. They depended on hand-me-downs and donations from the community to make ends meet.

According to the church historian, Reverend Wolff wore rebuilt shirts. When his collars became frayed from long-term wear, a seamstress in the congregation carefully cut out the collar, turned it upside-down so the frayed side would be underneath, and sewed the collar back in. That way, it would be good for another year.

The congregation, made up mostly of German farmers, provided Reverend Wolff and his family with virtually all their food. Reverend Wolff always had a milk cow. On his trips to Monthalia, he would take his sickle. On the way back after conducting services, he would cut Johnsongrass on the side of the road to feed his cow.

By the early 1940s, the congregation decided it was time to build a church. The site was St. Joseph Street, where the church still stands. They pledged $4,000 for a building contractor and 395 days of their own labor. Church members worked long and hard. One couple got involved in the task of removing dirt to accommodate the church basement. They lost track of time and worked until 2:00 a.m., then had to walk a mile and a half home. The next morning they were back on the job. The stucco building was completed in 1942. In 1947 the congregation bought a pipe organ for $2,900, only $1,100 less than what they paid the contractor for the building.

Reverend Wolff was called to another church in 1945. He was replaced by the Reverend W.H. Loeske. This man would have a significant influence on me at an impressionable time in my life. He blessed me by giving me a moral compass. I have misplaced it from time to time, but, thank God, there were people to help me find it. Reverend Loeske was the most dedicated, determined teacher I have ever had. He cared little about feelings. He taught with force and tenacity. His single-minded mission was to make his students good Lutherans for life.

Children were not allowed to take communion until after they had been confirmed, and confirmation required the successful completion of two years of catechism. The Reverend was not only a great pastor and teacher but also a great strategist. Before twelve-year-olds could enroll, their parents had to agree to support Reverend Loeske in his mission. He ran the course like Lutheran boot camp, drilling church history, doctrine, creeds, laws and responsibilities into the young recruits. He insisted that some of the fundamental material had to be memorized and recited in front of the congregation. In teaching, he had a Marine drill sergeant's mentality—he was looking for quality, not quantity. He believed the harder it was to join the church, the higher the honor.

Catechism classes were held in the church basement. They were supposed to last two hours but often lasted three. In the winter, we were told to bring plenty of clothes because the church couldn't afford to run the heater on Saturday. This was no problem to Reverend Loeske: he was in a teaching mode and oblivious to room or body temperature. In the late spring, the heat rose above the tolerable level. The more perspiration rolled down the Reverend's face, the longer he held us in bondage.

At the end of the second year, he dropped a bombshell: our class would not be confirmed because we had not fulfilled the basic requirements and did not deserve to be confirmed Lutherans. To my knowledge, no other class in the history of the church had ever flunked catechism. We were the first. My spiritual morale plummeted to an all-time low. The thought of spending another year of my Saturday afternoons in the church basement was almost unbearable. I was going on fourteen and my social demands were beginning to mount. But I had no choice. I did it because I had to, and today I'm glad I did.

So for a third year, we studied, memorized and recited. We shivered in January classes and sweated in May. When the class ended, Reverend Loeske pronounced us ready. For the confirmation ceremony, the girls wore lacy white dresses, and the boys wore white shirts and ties (first time for a necktie). Finally, we were real Lutherans.

Years later I became friends with a Lutheran pastor who had been a colleague of Reverend Loeske. My friend let me in on an inside joke about the fate of Lutheran pastors when they died. Those who fell short of their appointed mission had to spend a thousand years in purgatory teaching catechism to twelve- and thirteen-year-olds. My friend concluded: "Reverend Loeske would enjoy the tour of duty so much he would probably volunteer for an extension."

Easter Sunday was the day when everyone attended church services. Some of the attendees had not darkened the door of the church since the previous Easter. Reverend Loeske scorned that particular group. In his Easter message he referred to them as "Easter Christians." As the years went by, we had fewer Easter Christians at the service. Reverend Loeske was looking for potential members that were willing to commit.

The church always had an Easter egg hunt for the children. Since most of the members were farmers, chicken eggs were boiled and dyed for the hunt. A few candy eggs were contributed. To make the event more interesting, a one-dollar prize was awarded to the kid who found the most eggs. I was an aggressive hunter but never won the event. I was always hungry and always had an abundance of chicken eggs but never enough candy, so I ate the candy eggs as I found them and traded two chicken eggs for a candy one.

On Sunday Dad would give us a couple of pennies to put into the offering plate. The message was we all had a responsibility to support the church. Mom taught Sunday school and was active in the Ladies Aid Society. Reverend Loeske once used Mom's Bible as an example of how a Bible should look: dog-eared, well-used and worn.

Martin Luther founded the Lutheran Church on fundamental beliefs that demanded commitment and uncompromising goals from its members. Society has changed, but the mission of the church has remained the same. The members of the First Evangelical Lutheran Church have always cherished the moral absolutes they learned each and every week.

The First Evangelical Lutheran Church completed in 1942 for $4,000 and 395 volunteer days from the members.

Confirmation Sunday
After three years of catechism instruction under the tutelage of Reverend Loeske, we were too tired to smile. (I am on the second row, second from the right.)

My Best Friend

Pudge was my first dog. I was four and Sis was starting school—which would leave me home alone without a playmate. Our neighbor's dog had an unwanted litter, and the runt was just too cute for Mom to turn down. Pudge was the perfect name for this roly-poly, mixed-breed terrier, and he would soon become the perfect companion for me. Housebreaking Pudge was easy. He simply wasn't allowed inside. Mom did let me fix a bed for him in the smokehouse, so he was warm on those nights when the temperature dropped below freezing.

The spring after we got Pudge, we got his best pal, Butch. A friend had a rat terrier that needed a home. Butch and Pudge could have passed for brothers. Both stood about fifteen inches high and had athletic physiques, with long, lean muscles. Their bodies were covered with short, white hair with brown and black markings that shined in the sunlight. Their facial expressions were warm and friendly, but that could change quickly when duty called. During a crisis, their short, pointed ears would quickly turn back, indicating serious business was at hand. It was customary to crop a terrier's tail to about two inches approximately five days after birth. I didn't like the idea, but Dad assured me that it didn't hurt them at that age.

Raising small dogs offers a real advantage. They eat less than large dogs, and since we fed them table scraps, pickin's could be slim. When we threw the scraps out the back door, the food hardly hit the ground. Our hungry dogs would catch it in midair. Butch and Pudge would have made great Frisbee partners.

Our dogs were totally committed to protecting and pleasing our family. In return, we gave them praise and recognition for a job well-done. It's no wonder a dog is man's best friend. We could have had no better friends during the Depression than Butch and Pudge. They provided great companionship and unfailing loyalty to all of us.

Most dogs have fundamental virtues that often contribute to a person's mental health. They make good times better and bad times less difficult. They're always on top of their game with consistent, predictable behavior. It's jokingly said that the later you come home, the happier they are to see you. You never have to wait on them; they are ready around the clock. They never disagree and are always happy to share their time with you. Their loyalty is never in question. On a scale of one to ten, Butch and Pudge topped out with a score of ten.

We always had male dogs. Females had the possibility of adding more family members, which would mean more mouths to feed. Males never posed that problem. From time to time, however, they would get an urge to sow some wild oats and just disappear for a couple of days. Mom would say they "went prowling." It took me a while to understand what "prowling" meant. We had a large coyote population in the area. We seldom heard or saw them during the day, but we knew they were active at night. When our dogs returned limping and bleeding, it was clear they had encountered the coyotes. Our dogs would lie around for a few days, licking their wounds. It never occurred to Dad to take them to the vet. There was certainly no money for medical expenses for a dog, regardless of how much we loved them. We let them recover on their own, and they always did.

Stray dogs would also occasionally pose a problem. They would simply appear on our doorstep. We would run them off by various means, but they usually moved on anyway after realizing they couldn't get any food. Our dogs certainly were not inclined to share their scraps with strays. In fact, any attempt by a stray to impose on our dogs would result in a fight. There was barely enough for the home team to eat.

One year, Brother was raising turkeys as a moneymaking project. A pack of wild dogs attacked his turkeys, killing several. Luckily, Brother was nearby and quickly grabbed his shotgun. When the melee was over, the dogs disappeared into the woods and never returned.

Dogs in rural areas sometimes developed the habit of sucking out chicken eggs. Most farms had a few range chickens that got their food by eating grasshoppers and other insects. The chickens would lay their eggs in remote areas, under bushes and tall grass. If a dog got into the habit of finding the eggs before they were gathered, breaking the shells and sucking out the insides, he was a goner. Farmers couldn't afford the loss of the eggs, and there were no dog pounds around to take the dog. It was zero tolerance, usually a bullet between the eyes. Fortunately, our dogs never took up the habit.

Butch and Pudge served as our alarm system. We never had to worry about intruders, human or otherwise. The dogs would challenge anyone or anything that threatened the family—including snakes. Once I witnessed Butch and Pudge encircling a snake, much like a mongoose circles a cobra. When the snake wore out and lost its ability to strike with sufficient speed, Butch grabbed it behind the head. Pudge grabbed the other end. Then they played tug of war, pulling with all their strength until each had a bounty. At that point, they shook the remains and flung the entrails into the air.

One fatal day, Butch was bitten. We never knew if it was a rattlesnake or a copperhead, but the result was lethal. The bite on his belly exposed the flesh underneath. The area swelled so much that Butch could hardly move. We could see that he was dying. Dad made the difficult decision and asked our neighbor, Lonnie Smith, to take him to the corn patch. We all waited. At the sound of the gunshot, we shuddered. The whole family cried.

Pudge and I continued to be great friends. We spent many days playing together, just the two of us. Since I was isolated in the country with few playmates, Pudge became my best friend. He seemed to comprehend everything I told him. His only limitation was his inability to talk. Maybe that was best, since I shared many secrets with him. Our relationship was a classic example of a boy and his dog. Pudge lived a long, happy life.

One night before bedtime, when I was about fourteen, Dad told me it was time for Pudge to go. He was ten years old and too frail to continue living. I went out to the smokehouse and told him goodbye. I returned to bed, but for the first time in my young life, I was unable to sleep. The next morning Dad found me in Pudge's bed, both of us under the cotton-picking sacks. I slept well because I knew that we were doing what was best for Pudge. When I returned from school, Pudge was gone. I never asked for the details, but I knew Dad handled a difficult job well. Mom said I had to remember the cherished times Pudge and I spent together. I tried, but it took a long time to heal the pain in my heart.

Fur Trapping for Fun and Profit

About a mile from our house lay the lush San Marcos River bottom. Quiet and innocuous during the day, it came alive with activity as night fell. Coons, possums and other nocturnal creatures roamed about, searching for food and providing young boys with hours of fun and intrigue.

Brother and I were typical farm boys in the forties. Always trying to make a dollar whenever we could, we looked for ways to have fun while doing it. We spent many winters trapping animals and selling their skins. Winter was the best time of year for trapping because that's when the pelts were top quality. I, the perennial younger brother, served as an assistant (often a gopher) in the trapping process. That was OK by me because at least Brother let me participate. Trapping was for real men.

Fur was in vogue in the thirties and early forties. Movie stars and other celebrities were usually seen wearing fur coats and stoles and various fur-trimmed garments. Men in Gonzales responded to this demand by trapping small critters and selling their pelts. I don't remember any foxes in the area, but our river bottom was home to a few minks, and the woods had plenty of coons, possums and skunks—all marketable skins.

Prices fluctuated during the era of our enterprise. A possum pelt went from a low of twenty-five cents to two dollars, a coon for as much as five dollars, and a skunk from two to three dollars. As time went by, Brother started high school and grew out of the endeavor. When I was old enough to inherit the business, World War II had started and fashion took an austere turn. Furs were less in demand, and I missed the market.

Brother and I would start out in the late afternoon—looking quite macho, as I remember. Brother always led the way with his trusty .22 and the animal traps. I followed carrying a lunch (Mom insisted we take sausage sandwiches in a bucket in case we got hungry) and the bait for the traps. The bait consisted of salt pork and a variety of vegetables sure to please any varmint's palate.

As Brother and I approached the river bottom, we began scouting for fresh holes in the ground. We knew that possums and skunks dug holes for their homes and coons lived mostly in the tree hollows. Once we found a recently dug hole, we would secure the trap nearby.

We used metal spring traps handed down to us from Grandpa. Each was eight inches wide and twelve inches long and had a chain attached. We would set the trap in the most likely path of the possum or skunk at the entrance to its home; coon traps were set at the base of a tree hollow. We laid a chunk of salt pork on the trap and covered it with leaves. We slipped a peg in the last loop of the chain and drove the peg into the ground, or we attached the chain to a sturdy bush. That way, when the trap snapped shut, the animal could not run away with the trap.

By the time we set five or six traps, it was dark. We then hunted the coons and possums in the trees. Both of us had headlights, which resembled miners' headlamps, attached to our foreheads. We would scan the trees looking for two shiny eyes belonging to a possum or a coon. To shoot an animal in a tree at night with a .22 required great skill. I would often stand behind Brother shining the light down the top of the .22 barrel while he took dead aim. At age thirteen, Brother was a good shot. At age six, I wasn't even allowed to shoot the .22. I did keep the shells in my pocket and was constantly ready to re-arm him when necessary.

There's something exhilarating about being outdoors at night by yourself without parental guidance. We were invading a world dominated by creatures with keen night vision and hearing, and we had to be extra sharp to even think about challenging them on their own turf. I will never forget one November night in 1943. I was lagging behind Brother, probably because I was tired and cold, when I heard a shot pierce the silence. I immediately felt something drop on my back as it fell from the tree. I fell to the ground, thinking I'd been wounded. Brother ran back to me. He was shouting and laughing: a half-dead coon was clinging to my jacket. Not a funny experience by my way of thinking—but I can assure you, I kept an even pace with Brother from then on.

A few lucky people had coon dogs. We were not so fortunate. I never went on a hunt with dogs. I heard many times that if you shook a coon from a tree overhanging the river, you had better restrain your dog from going after the coon in the water. I don't know if this is true, but story has it that a coon can drown a dog. That would be a tragic loss because a good coon dog was valuable.

After a night of hunting, Brother and I would return the next morning to "run" the traps. If we had trapped a coon or possum, it was a simple process. We shot the animal and removed the trap. Skunks were more complicated. We had to shoot the skunk between the eyes for an instant kill before he sprayed his defensive fluid. Many times, he had already sprayed from the trauma of being trapped.

Either way, there was an odor problem. We buried the dead skunk for two or three days so the soil would absorb the odor. Then it was possible to skin the skunk and prepare the pelt for market.

Once a classmate of mine came to school after he had been sprayed. The teacher sent him home, saying: "The smell is a distraction. Don't come back until it's gone." He did smell strong. I wondered where he slept—probably in the barn. He had no fear, I'm sure, of any creature bothering him. Two or three days later, he returned to school. I guess the smell just wore off.

We brought the dead animals to the barn and removed their skins. With coons, we stretched the pelts and nailed them to the barn wall, the fur side facing the wall. Then we scraped the exposed hide with a knife until it was completely free of flesh and fat.

We handled skunk and possum pelts differently because they would shrink more than a coon's. We nailed two boards together at one end and pulled them apart slightly. Then we nailed the pelt across the two boards and continued pulling the boards apart until the pelt was stretched as tightly as possible. We nailed a third board to the bottom to hold the boards in place.

Brother and I were proud of those pelts, but we never quite made it to the trapping big leagues. Uncle Walter, on rare occasions, got a mink. Mink pelts went for twenty-five dollars apiece. Uncle Walter was a good hunter, tenacious and patient. He had another big advantage—he didn't have to go to school.

In early spring, the feed store in Gonzales would post a notice to let us know when the fur buyer would be in town. As we waited for his arrival, I would envision the new pair of tennis shoes or the upgraded set of marbles I was going to buy. For all the effort, we usually ended up with ten or twelve pelts that brought thirty or forty dollars.

After expenses (headlight batteries and .22 shells), my share would be five dollars, maybe six. Not bad for an intern. Far more rewarding was the education, adventure and bonding I experienced with Brother.

School Days

Brother entered the first grade in 1934 at the Diamond Grove School, a country school that was a mile from the house. His transportation was by horseback. The first few days, Dad escorted Brother and Sadie to school. After that, Sadie was put on autopilot. The journey was virtually risk-free; Sadie could barely walk and posed no danger of running away. Brother simply held on to the saddle horn and enjoyed the ride in the woods. Seven or eight horses and mules were staked out on the edge of the schoolyard, a scene that had not changed much since frontier days. One duty of the teacher was to loosen the horse's girth in the morning and cinch it up in the afternoon.

The dress of the day was bib overalls and shirts made from flour or feed sacks. Mom made certain the shirt was completely clean and neatly pressed. Brother carried his lunch in a syrup bucket.

The schoolhouse had two rooms and two teachers. Grades one through four were taught in one room and five through eight in the other. The building was just large enough to accommodate its sixty students. The uneven wooden floors and weathered walls creaked when the brisk winds blew in between the boards. Long tables served as desks and most assignments were completed on Big Chief tablets. Supplies were limited to the bare essentials.

Two wood stoves provided a minimal amount of heat during the winter. The eighth-grade boys were responsible for bringing in the wood every afternoon, and the teachers kept the fire going. The woodshed was out back between the boys' outhouse and the girls' outhouse. It's easy to see why the school year lasted only nine months. Summers were too hot and not conducive to learning. Besides, all the kids had to work in the field during harvest time.

Brother received a solid foundation, thanks to Mrs. Reid, an outstanding, dedicated educator. Mrs. Reid personified the saying "a teacher is forever." She would later be my first-grade teacher. She was a one-person Head Start program with no expense to the taxpayers.

Few students in country schools like Diamond Grove were expected to finish high school and virtually no one gave a thought to college. But all that changed when school busing made it possible for country schools to consolidate with the town schools. Town schools had an expanded curriculum, better qualified teachers and higher expectations. In 1938, when Brother was nine years old, he was bused into Gonzales. Town school placed new challenges on him, Mom and Dad. Bib overalls and syrup buckets were passé.

When the time came for me to start school, I attended Central Ward Elementary in town. I was continually reminded that I lived in the country. My shirts were either the neighbors' hand-me-downs or they were made of chicken-feed sacks. Mom usually could not afford the material to make me a real shirt, much less buy one in town. One day a group of the first-grade "town" girls taunted me by saying "cluck, cluck" as I walked past. I was humiliated. That night at dinner, I told Mom I couldn't wear those horrible shirts to school anymore. She had no comment, but I knew the answer. That was the end of the discussion. Sis and I got up from the table. She washed and I dried.

The student-teacher-parent relationship during the Depression was a simple one. The teachers had the freedom to teach without outside interference. Standards were set by the school system, and teachers were able to meet these standards without fear of lawsuits or court decisions.

There were no social promotions. Teachers would require a student to repeat a grade if necessary, without fear of reprisal from the parents. The school tried to accommodate all students from diverse backgrounds: aspiring collegians, potential vocational workers and those who had to drop out in order to work. A skilled teacher accomplished this by being sensitive and patient with the less gifted.

The same principles applied to discipline. The process was simple and straightforward. Any student causing a disruption in class would, without hesitation, end up in the principal's office. Punishment was swift and sure.

When I was ten, Mr. Jones became the elementary school principal. He had lived through the Depression and fought in World War II, making him a member of the "Greatest Generation." The lessons he learned and the philosophy he developed made him an outstanding school leader. He enforced discipline and made it possible for the teachers to devote their time and energy to teaching. He purposely kept a low profile during recess. When a situation arose, however, he was there in rapid order. He believed in the biblical philosophy that public punishment was the best deterrent against crime. He once caught three sixth graders behind the trash barrel smoking. Calmly, he asked another student nearby to go to his office and bring back his paddle. Mr. Jones ceremoniously disciplined the smokers, one by one, as the male student body looked on in silence. After that, no one ever thought about bringing a match or a cigarette to school.

It didn't take long for me to learn that I was wasting my time whining about some raw deal I got from my teacher or the principal. I knew my parents would side with the school. I once told Dad he had to hear my version of the story. His reply: "No, I don't." In other words, misbehaving and shirking responsibilities carried penalties. Furthermore, proper behavior didn't merit "good citizen" awards. Superficial praise was not passed out by parents, teachers and coaches. Rewards came only from accomplishment.

After the war, our nation was moving into a new era that demanded a higher standard of learning. The Gonzales school system rose to the challenge. It was a tremendous accomplishment for a farm kid to earn a college degree. Our schools made that dream a reality for those of us who were willing to make the commitment.

In elementary school, my favorite subject was recess. Many interesting dynamics emerged during this free time. The playground was where problems developed and where problems were solved. For the most part, Mr. Jones and our teachers left us to work things out for ourselves. During recess, the boys and girls played on separate playgrounds, divided by sidewalks in the front and rear of Central Ward. The girls controlled the sidewalks, however, because their activities included jacks and hopscotch. None of that mattered to me. What boy would want to participate in any of those sissy activities? When the girls' territory was violated, the intruder was quickly chastised by the rest of us. Occasionally, in defiance of rules and tradition, a thrill-seeking boy would dash through the girls' playground causing them to scream as if he were Jack the Ripper. What red-blooded American boy would not accept that occasional dare?

In addition to serving as principal, Mr. Jones doubled as our physical education teacher. Occasionally, he organized an activity such as softball and conducted a brief clinic on throwing, catching, batting and the basic rules of the game. Football was popular, and if we were lucky a classmate brought his ball from home. Only touch football was allowed. Getting tackled was painful when you hit the hardpan (packed dirt) of the schoolyard.

Other games included spinning tops and playing marbles. Marbles was a popular activity because it was competitive and cheap. The winner's prize was the loser's marbles. It never occurred to any of us that this could be considered gambling. There were occasional scuffles precipitated by such matters as using a stealie (an illegal marble). The fight was usually little more than pushing, shoving and rolling in the dirt. A punch was rarely thrown.

Another popular boys' game was mumbletypeg. In this game, players try to flip a pocketknife from various positions so that the blades would stick into the ground. Pocketknives were permitted in school because men and boys customarily carried them: they were a mark of manhood. Dad was never without his knife. It was handy for cutting rope and opening feed sacks. (It was also his manicure tool.) The Case brand was the Cadillac of pocketknives. On the other hand, switchblades were forbidden because they were thought to be deadly weapons. No one at Central Ward ever thought of using a pocketknife as a weapon. Our only weapon was a doubled-up fist.

In the spring of the sixth grade, a kid transferred in from I didn't know where and I really didn't care. He had a cocky demeanor, walking with his shoulders back and his chin in the air. He had a smart mouth and always appeared to be looking for trouble. I knew from the beginning that he was going to encroach on my turf. A couple of days was all it took for the line to be drawn in the sand. A crowd quickly gathered to witness the event. First I gave him a push and before he knew what had happened, I put him to the ground with a scissor trip. He jumped up and we exchanged more pushes and punches. During the melee, his fist found my eye and pain shot to the center of my brain. Before long, Mr. Jones appeared and broke up the fight. I later heard Mr. Jones was in no hurry to end the confrontation.

When I got back to class, I felt my eye. It was swollen. I had a shiner! I laid my head on the desk, faking a headache, concealing my humiliation. On the way home, I curled up on the back seat of the bus, continuing to fake my headache.

Facing Mom was my second confrontation of the day. Her reaction was predictable and perceptive. She understood boys were occasionally forced to fight, but she did not like the idea that her son would participate. I announced I could not go to school the next day. Her response was no surprise: "Yes, you will go to school. You made the bed, and now you sleep in it." Dad wanted to know the details when he came in from the field. As expected, he concurred with Mom. Sis, now an eighth grader, was too sophisticated to give the incident the dignity of a response. Thank goodness Brother was away at college; he would have really worked me over. My eye recovered before my ego, but time heals almost everything. I convinced myself it was a lucky punch. That rationalization helped speed the healing process. Recess was a great learning experience.

The classroom in town school provided a good environment for learning. Many of us started school with poor grammar and bad speaking habits. One of my teachers, Mrs. Bradley, accepted that challenge with unbridled determination. She made it clear that if we wanted to be successful we had to speak like successful people. She explained that even though our parents might not be speaking proper English, they wanted their children to do so. She devised a demerit system, enforced by fellow students, to break our poor speaking habits. Every time one of us used poor grammar, a classmate would call it to her attention and the speaker would receive a demerit. Peer pressure proved to be a successful strategy. Mrs. Bradley frequently reminded us that it was her job to stamp out ignorance. I will always be grateful to this tough, dedicated teacher. It's interesting that I never forget the tough ones.

Our educators relished the opportunity to improve our lives. Some teachers did not have a college degree; in fact, a few had little professional training. At that time, a person could obtain a teaching certificate by passing a state exam. There was no test for dedication, but my teachers scored high in that category. They were determined to make a difference.

In town school, our elementary studies included two extracurricular activities: music and art. The benefits I derived from them came only through osmosis. Mom (as mothers sometimes do) did not make an objective judgment when she insisted I pursue music. My starter instrument was a tonette, a cross between a clarinet and a flute. It was ten inches long and made of plastic. I learned how to run the scales but never could play anything. Mom would not give up. She borrowed a coronet, thinking my problem was caused by equipment failure. I was totally unable to play the coronet, so I tried the drums and then the baritone, all with the same results. I finally mustered up enough courage to tell Mom I was not born to be a musician. Standing up to Mom required a stiff backbone. I approached her as she worked at her sewing machine. Before I could force a word out, she saved me from the torture. "Buddy, I think you should concentrate on your studies and football and maybe try band later." I gave her a hug of gratitude and raced outside to find my football.

I remember two boys in my class who were academic superstars. One, Bobby Boothe, was especially good in band. He became a rocket scientist and spent many years working on the space program in Huntsville, Alabama. The other, Ernest Smith, can only be described as a bookworm. He received a law degree from Harvard and became a full professor and dean at the University of Texas Law School. We all knew those guys were smart but totally underestimated the level of their ability.

Today, almost on a daily basis, I reflect on the effort many people in Gonzales put forth to educate me. My parents would stop at nothing to support and encourage me in my endeavors, praise me in victory, sustain me during disappointing times and discipline me when necessary. After Dad had spent a twelve-hour day working in the field, and Mom had toiled at least twelve hours at home, both would be waiting at the school for my return from an out-of-town school activity. It was important to both of them to be there because they knew it was important to me. Until we got our new car in 1948, they often waited until nearly midnight in old Blackie, with only one window to shield them against the wind and a couple of quilts to keep them warm.

For my teachers, coaches and principals, teaching was far more than a job. It was a mission, fueled by dedication, to help this Depression boy from the country take on the world.

My twelve years of public education were spent in these three buildings.

Prejudice and Progress

Like many other parts of the nation in the 1940s, Gonzales was a community divided by prejudice. The ill treatment of minorities was commonplace during my younger years and continued for a considerable time thereafter. Gradually change occurred, some forced and some motivated by the conscience of the community. Young people, not yet set in their ways, knew that the prevailing attitudes were morally wrong. But change came slowly in our town.

The first blacks in the Gonzales area were slaves. They worked for cotton growers who built plantations in the rich bottoms of the San Marcos and Guadalupe rivers in the 1850s and early 1860s. After the Civil War, the prejudice against blacks continued to pass from generation to generation. I once asked Dad about the Ku Klux Klan that had been active in Gonzales in the 1920s but fortunately had declined in the '30s and early '40s. Dad just had one comment: "Good riddance." Dad had a problem expressing hate even for a hate organization.

Hatemongers were not visible in Gonzales the way they were in parts of the South and even in other parts of Texas, but the predominant public position was that black people were all right as long as they stayed in their place. For the most part, they lived out of sight and out of mind. They existed in the community but stayed to themselves. They went to their own schools, stores, barbershops and doctors. They were ill-prepared for jobs and were relegated to manual labor and menial work because they were denied a proper education. Although they were treated better in Gonzales than in other regions of Texas and the Deep South, blacks still suffered harsh discrimination.

All of this was really hard for me to comprehend when I was eight years old. At the time, a neighbor employed a black family with a boy my age. His father performed outdoor tasks, and his mother was the housekeeper. Their name was White. The boy, also named Buddy, became my playmate. Since he was Buddy White, he began to call me Buddy Black. We both thought that was great fun. I have fond memories of the adventures of Buddy White and Buddy Black. We spent many hours fishing in the creek and hanging out together. Once I invited him to come home with me for lunch. He refused, and I didn't really understand why. Later Mom told me he probably felt uncomfortable coming to a white person's house. This made me sad. I didn't see Buddy White much after that.

A short time later a violent spring thunderstorm swept through the area. A neighbor came to report that the Whites' house had almost blown down and asked if Dad would help repair it. The entire Schrader family responded. When we arrived at the scene, the rickety little house was barely standing. The men cut four thick mesquite posts, dug deep holes at the corners of the house and placed the poles in the ground. They tied ropes around the house, and our mules slowly pulled the structure toward the poles, securing it back to its original position. The poles served as anchors to keep the house in place. Thanks to a well-thought-out plan, a strong mule team and help from neighbors, the Whites could feel a bit safer during violent storms. I was gratified to know that we had helped my friend and his family in their time of tragedy. I also came to realize why Buddy might have felt ill at ease in our "fancy" home.

While I was growing up in Gonzales, the public schools were segregated. We had Gonzales High School for whites and Edwards High School for blacks. By the time the U.S. Supreme Court decided in 1954 that school segregation was unconstitutional, I had left for college. Most of the time I was in school in Gonzales, I didn't think much about segregation. But there were times that it was hard to ignore.

The first time I saw the "Chicken Coop," I was five years old and on my way up the road toward the mailbox. A Model T Ford-type bus drove by, sputtering and spewing black smoke. The vehicle with its peeling paint and broken-out windows appeared to be at least twenty years old. I will never forget the small, black faces peering down at me through the chicken wire. I later learned that the windows had been covered with the wire to protect the children from other kids outside who were throwing rocks at them. I could usually hear the old bus coming for miles, since it had no muffler. When the contraption drove by, clattering and banging, the white kids would snicker and laugh. On days when the rattletrap bus would not run at all, which was often, the kids simply didn't go to school. I knew this just wasn't right. I didn't want to ride in their dirty, old bus, and yet I didn't feel like I should be riding in such a shiny, new one either. My parents had taught me to treat everyone equally, and yet society was setting different standards. I never could reconcile the conflict.

Years later, when I was in the army stationed at Fort Hood, one of the guys who used to ride on the "Chicken Coop" recognized me and introduced himself. He was from a well-respected black family, and all his brothers and sisters had graduated from college. We became good friends at Fort Hood, and over time I learned the struggles he endured. He was not looking for sympathy or praise; he simply shared his story with me. He compared his childhood experiences to those of a soldier in combat. It was tough, he said, but he had the "big guns" (his parents) for support. They made him "combat ready" with training and discipline and never allowed him to fall into self-pity. In the process of growing up, he developed the most important tool for survival: self-determination. When he rode on the "Chicken Coop," it was just another "round of artillery" coming at him. He knew he was going to survive. Looking back, I think the skills he used to endure racism were the same skills I was taught to endure the Depression. I know his challenges were greater than mine, but I could relate to his struggle.

Mexican-Americans lived in a small section of town on the west side. Many of these families were poorly educated and spoke little or no English. The children attended Riverside Elementary, an all-Spanish school. After the sixth grade, they entered the town's only junior high school, but their limited English skills made learning difficult. Most dropped out in junior high or high school. In my high school graduation class, I remember that only six of the seventy-three students were Hispanic. One Latino classmate made it on the varsity football team as a running back. Although he was never a star, he managed to withstand the hazing and make a significant contribution to the program.

Discrimination can take many forms. When Brother transferred to Central Ward Elementary School in town, the grades were divided: there were classes for the country kids and classes for the city kids. Brother was put into the country kids' class. Classes for country kids had less capable teachers, fewer supplies and lower expectations. But Brother was a serious student, the teacher liked him and he made good grades. As a result, he was moved into the city class in the sixth grade. Many country kids were not so lucky.

When I started to school in 1942, the first grade did not have separate classes for country and city kids, as best I can remember, but we did have various forms of social discrimination. Strangely, one form was based on a student's lunch container. The lowest social class, usually consisting of poor, rural kids, used syrup buckets to carry their lunches to school. Often the buckets contained only cornbread and molasses. I remember one classmate who always had catsup sandwiches that got so soggy he couldn't hold the bread.

The next rung of the social ladder were the kids who brought lunch wrapped in newspaper tied with string. When we could, my family bought a newspaper after church on Sunday, so I often used it to carry my lunch. This group of rural kids was only slightly less poor than the "bucket brigade."

One step above the newspaper wrap was the brown paper bag. Those in this more fortunate group had new, wrinkle-free bags that were used exclusively for the child's lunch. I was caught between the second and third level. Sometimes there was a brown bag available for my lunch, but never a crisp, new one. My lunch bags were used grocery sacks. I wanted to remain in the second tier, so I would neatly fold the rumpled brown bag, put it into my hip pocket and take it home for re-use.

The most affluent kids in the class carried metal lunchboxes. The boys' lunchboxes were mostly solid silver or black, but some were fancy with pictures of heroes such as Roy Rogers and Flash Gordon. The girls' kits had brightly colored cartoon characters like Mickey and Minnie Mouse and Cinderella. Inside these glamorous containers were crust-free sandwiches made of lunchmeat and store-bought bread, fresh fruit, cookies and, in some cases, a matching Thermos filled with milk or fruit punch. All the food items were neatly wrapped in wax paper. Despite this ostentatious display of wealth, these kids were always willing to trade me a Baby Ruth or a Butterfinger for one of Mom's homemade kolaches. In my mind, that somehow elevated me to their level.

Social standing was also conveyed by the way we dressed. In elementary school I often wore shirts made of chicken-feed sacks, and kids living in town wore store-bought clothes. But throughout school, my parents insisted that we show dignity and pride in our appearance. "Tuck in your shirttail," Mom would say. Our shirts were always clean and pressed. "Don't go around looking sloppy," she insisted.

We applied the same dignity and pride to our home, basic as it was. We seldom envied those who were better off. We simply hoped one day we could have some of the things they possessed. My parents believed that education was the path to a better life and that everyone deserved an opportunity to succeed.

Today I believe America is stronger, Gonzales is stronger and I am stronger than I was fifty years ago because we are treating each other with kindness, compassion and respect. We are all better people and feel better about ourselves. We are still a work in progress.

Entertainment

Brother, Sis and I spent many summer evenings chasing lightning bugs. We used to have contests to see who could catch the most and, more important, whose bugs could live the longest. Mom made sure we were especially careful with the Mason jars she let us use as bug containers. They had to be used later in canning her famous dill pickles.

During the Depression, the adults never had to worry about whether their children were being entertained. Kids back then had to be creative. They invented their own games while their parents sat in the shade of the backyard trees, sipped a cool drink and shared thoughts, hopes and dreams. They told the same stories of the past over and over again with a little different twist each time. During these difficult years, the well-being of relatives and friends was paramount on everyone's mind. These evenings of "visiting" were a crucial means of sharing news and socializing for many rural families. In the early and mid-forties news of the war dominated most conversations.

Churches in Gonzales, as in most small American towns, were social gathering places for the community. Churches held revivals and retreats on the church lawn, complete with an abundance of homemade vegetables, breads, cakes and pies. Kids played kick-the-can or hide-and-seek, ladies scurried around setting out the food, and the men sat together smoking roll-your-own cigarettes. The highlight of every revival was the visiting preacher's forceful, emotional message to the crowd. Some churches held prayer meetings followed by covered-dish suppers on Wednesday nights. Sunday mornings were for Sunday school and worship. These events filled a vital spiritual and social need in the community. They brought families together and provided a means for neighbors to share in each other's lives.

Families occasionally gathered on Saturday night at one of the local dance halls. Mothers and fathers always brought all the children, and the children often did most of the dancing. A group of local musicians would play—typically a combination of German, Czech and country-western tunes. On cold nights, mothers would lay their babies on pallets in front of the wood-burning stoves. Sometimes, there were as many as twenty babies nestled on those makeshift beds. I often wondered if a parent ever took home the wrong baby.

The Gonzales "country club" was Mundrick's, a domino hall on Confederate Square, next to Michelson's Cafe. The hall was an all-male club, providing a robust atmosphere for gaming, gossiping and bonding. It was probably much like today's country club, but not quite as classy. The absence of a feminine touch was evident in the rugged wood bar, wobbly old tables and chairs, and layers of grit and grime on the tobacco-stained floor. A constant haze of cigarette smoke and the smell of rancid beer hung in the air, undoubtedly the result of poor housekeeping and lack of ventilation. At that time, public buildings didn't have to meet fire codes or health department standards. Maybe this was all part of the grand scheme. No woman, regardless of social standing, would dare darken the door of this place. Mom said the smell was so bad she had difficulty just walking by.

When I was about twelve years old, a lady standing outside the hall asked me to give a message to her husband that it was time to go home. I was excited about making my first venture into the club. The loud talk, vulgar language, and the dominoes slamming against the table on critical plays all added to the intrigue. I approached Slats, the bartender, and asked him to give Mr. Richie the message. Mr. Richie left right away.

The cost of a round of dominoes was ten cents, or two and a half cents a person. But dominoes were just the bait for holding the clients captive. The lifeblood of the business was the profit from the sale of Lone Star, Pearl, Jax, Grand Prize and Shiner beer. One day, returning from the hall, Grandpa Vackar wrecked his car. He hit a parked vehicle and narrowly escaped serious injury. The family firmly but compassionately took away his keys. Grandma was convinced he had exceeded his two-beer limit. Grandpa Vackar vehemently denied the accusation but lost his case. Her suspicion was legitimate; he was coming home more than an hour late. Strangely, the wreck added some quality years to Grandpa's life. Five days a week, he had to walk the mile and a half to the hall. The walk exercised his body, the dominoes kept his mind active and the camaraderie kept alive his competitive spirit and social contacts.

On warm summer days, kids would spend hours at one of the many swimming holes along the Guadalupe and San Marcos rivers. The town favorite was Santa Anna Ford on the Guadalupe, south of town. At the home place Dad attached a rope to a large cypress tree that hung over the San Marcos River, and that was the only equipment we needed to entertain ourselves. The competition revolved around who could swing on the rope the most number of times before his arms gave out and he had to fall in. I never could keep up with Brother, but at least he let me have a turn.

One August afternoon, I was elected to climb that cypress to adjust the rope to accommodate the lower river level. I shimmied up the tree trunk and crawled out on the limb, with my attention focused on finding the rope while holding onto the limb. Suddenly, I came face to face with a cottonmouth moccasin. That gray-black snake, about three feet long, was stretched out on the limb, its white mouth open, less than a foot away. I screamed and jumped into the river. I have no idea what happened to the snake, but I never climbed that tree again. It was probably the closest encounter with near death I ever had as a child.

The same year I encountered the moccasin was also a prolific year for wasps. One day a friend in my third-grade class came to our house with his mother. Mom was making a dress for her, so he and I played outside while they conducted business. We thought it would be fun to knock down the yellow-jacket nests that were covering the eaves of the smokehouse and the barn. At first we used sticks. With a whack, the nest would fall and the wasps would fly out. Outrunning them seemed easy, so we abandoned the stick method and just used our hands. The object of the game was to see who got stung the least! Fortunately, neither of us was allergic, but upon hearing the story, Mom insisted we find something else to occupy our time. Brother was not impressed. He said my underarm odor was attracting the infuriated insects. I didn't think he was right, but I did begin sneaking his Old Spice deodorant stick when he wasn't home.

Radio was a welcome change from "visiting," and I was always excited when Dad would let us listen. The radio allowed the family to escape into fantasy lands that were limited only by our imagination. We listened to *The Lone Ranger*, *The Shadow*, *Flash Gordon*, *Amos 'n' Andy* and *Fibber McGee and Molly*. *Dr. I.Q.* was the forerunner of modern-day TV quiz shows. I remember one of his trick questions: "On which side of the cup is the handle?" The answer: “the outside.” (I never got those questions right.) *Meet the Press* began on the radio as did comedians such as Jack Benny, Bob Hope and Red Skelton. These shows were classic examples of some of the best talent our country has ever produced. I am fortunate that they were a part of my childhood.

The Saturday afternoon picture show was the best entertainment value of the Depression. The admission for kids younger than twelve was twelve cents. For that price, you could enjoy a double-feature movie, a serial, a cartoon and previews for the next week’s coming attraction, all in the comfort of air conditioning (one of the few air-conditioned buildings in town). This took care of the kids while the parents shopped and socialized on the courthouse square.

One of the movie features was often a western shoot-’em-up. The star was macho, smart, tough and always victorious. Against all odds, just when the outlaws thought they had the upper hand, the hero would outsmart the villains and bring them to justice. The other half of the double feature was often a horror movie such as *The Wolfman*, *Frankenstein* or *Dracula*.

The serials were fast-moving films, full of adventure and unbelievable feats. Many times the last scene found the hero in a hopeless state of impending doom. We had to wait until the next Saturday to see if he escaped defeat or death.

I once asked Brother if everything we saw at the movies was true. He couldn’t pass up the opportunity to have a little fun, so he assured me it was all factual. The next Dracula movie left me horrified. I had nightmares for months. I guess I was lucky we didn’t have a lot of extra money to spend at the theater. I remember only one movie we saw as a family. I was about five years old, and the movie starred John Wayne. He made a lasting impression on me at that young age.

By far, the biggest social event of the year was the county fair. Held in October at the end of the harvest season, the fair was the time for everyone to exhibit their finest accomplishments. The weekend festivities started with a parade that wound through the downtown streets of Gonzales. The fair was considered so important that the community declared the first day, a Friday, a school holiday. After all, many kids were entering a prize bull, pig or rooster in the livestock competition. Students also participated in essay contests and rodeo events.

The fair was appropriately named the Gonzales County Fair and Pecan Exposition. Pecans were in abundance at that time of year, and competition for the sweetest nut was fierce. The pecans came from native as well as grafted trees. The hundred-year-old native pecan trees along the Guadalupe River bottom were prolific; they produced large crops of delicious nuts that were shipped all over the country.

The Schraders did quite well at the fair every year. In 1940, Brother won for best handwriting in his grade and gender group. (It would be unfair for the boys to compete with the girls.)

Mom walked away with the blue ribbon in the quilting competition. She always had an abundance of sewing scraps, so her quilts were unique and colorful. For Mom and other women during the Depression, quilting was an ongoing social event, a time to gather and share scraps and news of the day. The only cost was thread. Cotton from the fields provided the batting for the inside, and scraps of sewing fabric, flour sacks and even old clothes provided the fabric for the outside. It was an example of getting the squeal out of the pig. A neighbor on the Foster place once made a quilt out of Bull Durham tobacco pouches. The family was pitifully poor, yet they had enough money for tobacco. Amazing.

Grandma Vackar often won first place in the baking division for her homemade kolaches. I will never forget the tables crowded with pies, cakes and cookies. The judges in this event always looked as though they had eaten one piece of cake too many. Most judges came from out of town because it was far too political to judge the entries of your friends and relatives.

The fair provided something for everyone. A traveling carnival always set up at the far end of the fairgrounds. Bumper cars, a Ferris wheel, a shooting gallery and ring-toss games were among the many amusements. One year the carnival proprietor added a new special attraction: a peep show. (It amounted to three scantily clad young women who performed a poor version of the hula.) Local religious groups succeeded in closing down the show after the first night.

County fairs were also popular venues for traveling road shows. One such traveling show was that of W. Lee "Pappy" O'Daniel. He ran for Texas governor (and won) in 1938 and 1940; he served in the U.S. Senate and tried for a comeback as governor in the 1950s. He campaigned by traveling the state with a fold-out stage and entertaining the townsfolk with an afternoon of singing and "speechifying." A popular band, the "Light Crust Doughboys," campaigned with him and made quite a name for themselves.

Most traveling shows had an unsavory reputation. The town fathers wouldn't allow the shows to set up on the main square, so the show often performed behind the cotton mill in an area known as "Foggie Flats." Typically the show arrived in a Model A truck, which served several purposes: it provided transportation, it could be quickly transformed into a stage and it served as sleeping quarters for the performers. I remember one show in particular that had three performers. A woman, wearing bright red lipstick and a skirt shorter than those of any woman I knew, played the accordion. In the background a middle-aged man played the banjo. I could tell from the vacant look in his eyes that he was probably mentally retarded. The star, of course, was the "doctor"—complete with goatee, tuxedo and black patent leather shoes. He peddled his various products as miracle cures, but I suspect they were mostly alcohol. He sold snake oil, which supposedly was derived from an Egyptian plant (with crooked roots) and was designed to cure hypertension and depression. The doctor made a huge profit on his merchandise and passed around a large fruit basket for donations to the entertainers. The basket was usually full, and the good doctor and his supporting cast returned to Gonzales year after year.

For several years, a roller-skating rink came to town and stayed for a couple of weeks. The flooring was stacked in sections on a flatbed truck. When unloaded and laid out, the rink was about the size of a basketball court. A tent sprawled overhead. Young adults and children would rent skates and skate around while others watched from the sidelines. When it first arrived, the rink was a novelty, and skaters and spectators alike made it the place to be. When the rink lost its bloom, the business would pack up and move to another town. I never skated because the chance of falling down and humiliating myself in front of the girls was far too risky.

A circus stopped in Gonzales every summer. It had the usual array of circus animals, trapeze artists, freaks, sideshows and rigged midway games. The community always enjoyed the fun and excitement, until the Dailey Brothers Circus decided to make Gonzales its winter headquarters. It was said that this troupe chose our town so they could bathe in the Guadalupe but then discovered that the water was too cold. They spent those months in Gonzales much like refugees from a Third World country, much to the disgust of the local citizens. Before leaving in the spring, the performers did give us a parade through downtown. Unfortunately, business owners were left to clean up the animal waste, including the elephant droppings, which were sizeable. For days, the town square smelled like a livestock auction barn. That was the first and last time the circus wintered in Gonzales, but they continued to return year after year to lift our spirits.

I suppose it sounds strange to say we were never bored, but we never were. The hours we spent by ourselves were filled with make-believe and inventiveness. Boys played cowboys and Indians, built forts and fought imaginary enemies. Girls played house and raised their dolls on mud pies and tender, loving care. Times were simpler then and in many ways, just maybe, they were better.

Crystal Theatre
The best entertainment bargain in town and one of the few air-conditioned buildings.

The Circus was touted as the "Greatest Show in Gonzales."

The Gonzales County Fair and Pecan Exposition

The great event opened with a parade on the square. The occasion was so big, it was a school holiday.

Wholesome family entertainment.

A great display of talent, pride and hard work.

Domino Hall
For Men Only
Gonzales' answer to a country club.

Santa Anna Ford on the Guadalupe River. The rope swings hanging from the giant cypress trees help make it a great swimming hole.

Fred: My Champion Pig

In the seventh grade, I joined the 4-H Club. My interest was sparked after I had written a winning essay on the care of a Jersey heifer. The project, sponsored by Gonzales State Bank, not only challenged me but also increased my sense of responsibility to our farm. When the heifer, Mindy, came of age, she produced a calf that was donated to the club. Mindy merged into our herd and developed into a productive milk cow. I was proud of my contribution to the school program and to our farm.

My eighth-grade 4-H project was to raise and show a Duroc hog. We went to a local farmer who specialized in champion show hogs and looked at pigs that had been weaned a week earlier. I chose the most alert and slickest—the pick of the litter. I named him Fred.

One rule of the project was that I could not abdicate the duties and responsibilities for the animal's care. When the time came for castration, however, Dad had to perform the surgery. I did not have the heart, skill or stomach to take a knife to Fred. It was hard enough to hold him down for the procedure. The surgery was a success, which meant that Fred could get focused on his objective in life: to win a prize at the hog shows.

Fred grew up to be a beautiful physical specimen: great body conformation and well-disciplined with a good temperament, which was essential for show animals. We won the first round of competition in the Gonzales County area. Then we were off to the regional contest in San Antonio. I didn't know if it was legal, but I applied a dab of my Vaseline Hair Oil on Fred's thick, red coat so it would shine under the bright lights of the judging arena. I was worried Dad would find out and turn me in.

The regional event was held at a livestock show barn in San Antonio. I was excited. If Fred won, we would be in the state finals the next month at the San Antonio livestock show. A win also meant that I could go to the rodeo.

The big day arrived. It was the biggest day in Fred's life and the second biggest in mine. (By that time, I was playing football, and the previous November we had beaten the Lockhart Lions in the last play of the game.) Dad and I were up and ready before daylight. Shortly afterward, Uncle Otto arrived in his Chevy pickup. We left early in case of truck trouble and allowed for the possibility of getting lost. We weren't about to take the chance of being late. Rubber was on the road at 7:00 a.m., which allowed us four hours for an hour-and-a-half trip.

Just out of Belmont, Uncle Otto felt something unusual in the Chevy's steering system. He pulled over and, sure enough, we had a flat. Dad reminded me how wise it was to allow for emergencies. In fifteen minutes we were back on the road motoring toward Seguin and admiring the beautiful farmland along the Guadalupe River bottom. I checked Fred every ten minutes. He seemed to be enjoying the ride; the breeze blowing in his face gave him a half smile.

Just past Seguin on Highway 90, we stopped at the Elite Cafe and Truck Stop. The cafe was a few levels below elite, but it looked pretty fancy to me. I had never eaten breakfast in a cafe. We dropped off the flat at the filling station while we ate. I was impressed with the cafe's macho environment. Muscular truck drivers, wearing cowboy boots, big belt buckles and wide-brimmed hats, convinced me that nobody ever messed with them. Dad was provoked when he spotted a driver wearing his hat while he was eating. No one would ever do that in Gonzales. I just thought how great it would be to grow long sideburns like theirs. Maybe I could even pick up a few tips on how to flirt with a waitress!

We picked up our tire and were soon back on the road. We were again taken by the beautiful farmland between Seguin and San Antonio. Dad commented that the good earth was resting and getting ready to go to work in a couple of months. I was impressed: God's country extended beyond Gonzales.

In San Antonio, we hung a right off Highway 90 and made it to the show barn without incident. Judging began in the main arena at 11:00 a.m. There were twenty nonchalant hogs and twenty anxious boys, all looking for one prize, first place. The boys had swagger sticks, buggy and jockey whips and cut-off walking canes as aids to direct their prized animals during the judging. I felt intimidated with my mesquite stick, even though I had removed the bark and varnished the wood. I hoped the inferior equipment would not count against me.

The judging took a long time. Two judges examined the animals and eliminated the contestants one by one. After what seemed to be hours, two beautiful hogs were left in the arena: Fred and one other Duroc. I tried to be cool but my heart was pounding. I was one competitor away from being in the Super Bowl of 4-H hog competition. Then it happened. The judge ran his finger under a small spot of hair on the right side of Fred's rump. Then I understood why the judge had a wrap of white tape on his finger. He had discovered a patch of black hair, no bigger than a pencil eraser. As many times as I had washed and groomed Fred, I had never noticed the imperfection. Prize Durocs must be all red. The judge nodded his head toward the exit gate and gave me a pat on the shoulder. Fred was disqualified because of a minute genetic flaw.

Returning home, we rode in silence until we were near Seguin. Dad, in his slow, deliberate way of talking, said, "Son, there are times when more is learned in defeat than in victory." I didn't understand what he meant. In fact, had I not respected him so much, I would have thought he was making a stupid remark. Uncle Otto put his arm around me and gave me a hug. Looking back at Fred, I couldn't be mad. It wasn't his fault he had a birth defect.

When we arrived home, I went straight to my room because I didn't want anyone to see me cry. As usual, Mom did the perfect thing: she helped by sharing a cry with me. Dad came by and said Fred needed his supper. I guess he was telling me, win or lose, Fred was still my friend and I needed to take care of him. Fred was totally unaffected by the event. He ate his slop with as much enthusiasm as ever. Pudge showed his support by going to the barn with me, and I slowly recovered.

The next Saturday, Uncle Otto took Fred to the auction sale. I was sad to see him go. Fred and the 4-H Club did their job by giving me an "A" in the school of hard knocks. I knew I wasn't going to be a dirt farmer, a rancher or a pig farmer, so I gave up 4-H. When Brother entered Texas Tech, my focus turned to college, but 4-H had been a great partner in my education.

Mindy was a good 4-H project and later provided an abundance of milk for the family.

The owner of the feed store gave me this sign when Fred won the county competition. On to San Antonio!

Friday Night Fever

In 1944 when the Apaches won the district football championship, Gonzales broke out with "Friday night fever." The victory served as a welcome break from the horrible war news that dominated our town.

The next year, when Brother began his junior year in high school, he decided to try out for football. That was strange and scary news for Mom and Dad. They had never even seen a football game. All they knew was that it was a rough affair, and the object was to knock people down! In the process, they surmised, most participants got hurt, many maimed for life.

Brother had a selling job to do. He brought his uniform home, complete with full pads and helmet, to demonstrate that the game was not nearly that dangerous. Brother performed various blocks on the peach trees by the kitchen window. He hit the tree hard with a shoulder block, a cross-body block and a reverse-scissor block. Then he butted the tree with his helmet. Not convinced, but having seen enough of the foolishness, Mom and Dad acquiesced. Brother was on his way to a football career.

At age sixteen, Brother had developed a big, strong, athletic body. He made the Apache starting lineup his first year. Mom and Dad had yet to go to a game. They were still prejudiced against the sport and hoped the phase would pass. I wanted to see a game, so one Friday night I caught a ride with a neighbor. For me, at age nine, the crowd and the noise were exciting. Four or five hundred people filled the stands—the largest gathering I had ever seen. I heard my brother's name called over the loudspeaker when he got a tackle. I decided I liked this sport. "Someday I'm going to play football," I thought. At the half, I assumed the game was over and found my ride. When they informed me we still had another half to go, I was delighted. I didn't know then, but the decision I made that night would change my life.

When I was eleven, a friend invited me to go to the varsity game in Seguin: the Apaches vs. the Seguin Matadors. But there was a problem. Seven people would have to ride in the family's '37 Chevy. My friend's parents would not let their son renege on the invitation, so one of his older brothers volunteered to ride the thirty miles on the running board. He made it just fine, standing on the outside of the car with his arm looped around the door posts. I imagine he closed his mouth to avoid bug spatter on his teeth. We won the game and he forgot about the potential bug problem, smiling all the way home and savoring the victory.

Before radio station KCTI (CTI stands for Cradle of Texas Independence) began broadcasting Apache football games, several local characters competed fiercely to be the first to deliver the scores of the out-of-town games to the fans waiting on the courthouse square. Those Paul Revere types felt they were performing a valuable community service. One particular Friday night, two drivers raced home from the game to deliver the happy tidings: Apaches 14, Lockhart Lions 7. It's possible these two might have overindulged in Lone Star or a flask of Jim Beam because one of them flipped his car several times. He somehow managed to walk away from the wreckage and hitch a ride to Gonzales. To his dismay and disappointment, his competitor had delivered the good news fifteen minutes earlier. An old Gonzales adage again proved to hold some truth: "The Good Lord takes care of drunks and idiots."

Brother had a great senior year. Even though he weighed only 180 pounds, he had ambitions to try out at some college and get a football scholarship. This was an opportunity, perhaps a ticket out of the cotton patch. Mom and Dad realized they needed to understand this game. It had become a significant part of their son's life. They learned to embrace the sport and wholeheartedly supported Brother's participation.

In the spring of 1947, when I was in the fifth grade, Brother made his college plans. He was going to Texas Tech in Lubbock because his best friend was going there and he could get a ride—400 miles from home. Brother got a half scholarship the first semester. With the money he had saved from his summer job and $125 from the folks (leaving Dad's bank balance at $50), he made it through the first semester. Three and a half years later, he graduated from Trinity University in San Antonio. Football had paid for his college education

While Brother was planning for college, I went to my first spring training for the junior high school team, the Papooses. As a fifth grader, I could try out for the "B" team. I sent word via Sis that I would not be coming home on the bus because I had football practice. I would worry later how to get home. I was consumed by my objective: football. After practice, I ended up at Grandma Vackar's house and waited for the folks. From then on, Grandma's house was the rendezvous point. Grandma always managed to prepare a home-cooked meal, usually fresh vegetables and sausage from our farm. She was an incredible cook.

My coach was the junior high P.E. instructor, an official looking, authoritative figure. His shorts were at least two sizes too small, and his T-shirt stretched over his midsection, accentuating an oversized stomach. He seemed quite proud of what he perceived was a great athletic physique. The frayed bill of his baseball cap showed many seasons of wear, and the crown was soaked with oil (probably from heavy-duty hair tonic). He spoke loud and fast, his voice filled with emotion; he was determined to put fire into the bellies of his young recruits. Every time he began a sentence, he spat a stream of chewing tobacco. He must have been a levelheaded man because tobacco juice escaped from both edges of his mouth in equal amounts. Whenever he looked at me, I developed a near fatal case of intimidation. When he spoke, I froze.

The uniform I was given was designed to fit a varsity player weighing at least 150 pounds. I didn't weigh half that much. I suspect the equipment had seen better days in the early thirties. My pants housed kneepads and thigh pads. The kneepads were supposed to end just below my kneecaps, but they made it down to my ankles. The thigh pads came down to my knees. The rest of the uniform, the hip pads, shoulder pads and jersey, was consistent with the lower-body fit. My leather helmet still had a hard crown, but the ear flaps were so worn that you could fold them completely under. I surmised that a wide-rumped interior lineman had sat on it. The snaps that secured the chin strap were missing so I couldn't use it. The helmet was so large that I could spin it around on my head. This head gear provided little protection from cranial injury or brain damage, but it beat playing without a helmet (I guess). I suspect it did lower my IQ.

The first practice drill was calisthenics. It consisted of stretching, conditioning and body building. I did pretty well with sit-ups, push-ups and touch-the-toes-without-bending-the-knees. The one I had a problem with was the side-straddle hop. This required more coordination than I possessed. I was supposed to hop, spread my legs and swing my arms over my head, in one continuous, rhythmic motion.

Thank goodness I finally got the hang of it. Failure to master this skill, I feared, might mean missing the first cut.

After calisthenics, it was time for the rubber to meet the road, or said another way, time to separate the boy scouts from the cub scouts. This activity was the head-on tackling drill. Two single-file lines of recruits faced one another, approximately ten yards apart. The object was to carry the football and run head-on into the first person in the other column, while that person tried to tackle you. Only real men qualified.

When it was my turn to be the tackler, I was astonished to see that the ball carrier I was facing, ten yards directly in front of me, was a large seventh grader. He was Sis' classmate, a big bully type. At the time he looked like an NFL linebacker. As he took the ball, he started laughing at me. That added to the intimidation. The coach recognized the mismatch and ordered me to step aside to avoid death or dismemberment. I was already in my three-point stance prepared for combat and refused. I glanced up and saw Brother standing under a large oak tree, watching me. Everyone knew he was headed to Texas Tech in the fall to play football. Coach again ordered me to step aside, and again I refused. I had to do it. If I didn't, I would be cut from the team on the spot and Brother would be embarrassed. There was no backing down now. The coach gave me a look that said, "Well, OK, but you may die," and shouted "Hike" to the seventh-grade lug. My survival instinct told me to turn tail and run, but I didn't. I crouched to take the blow. My shoulder pad hit the bruiser's legs perfectly square. Whump! We both hit the ground hard. I got up fast, feeling good about what I had done. The ball carrier got up slowly, shaken and certainly not laughing. Brother came over and slapped me on the shoulder pad, "Nice tackle!" he said. I never felt better in my life. I loved this game. Nothing would ever be the same.

During my junior high years, I had an obsessional fear that I would never be big enough to play center or linebacker in college. My classmates were getting taller and heavier. The more I worried, the more I ate. Finally, between the ninth and tenth grades, I grew six inches and gained fifty pounds. Dad said he could have fed three hogs with the food I consumed.

One fellow on the Papoose team stands out in my memory. He was a couple of years ahead of me and played tailback, the key position in the single-wing formation. He came from a large family—eight brothers and sisters—and I know he often went to bed hungry. No one ever remembered him wearing shoes to school, so the assumption was he had none. One Friday night in November, it was so cold that our coach found a pair of shoes for him to wear during the game. At halftime, we were losing, 18 to 0. The coach desperately tried to rally his boys and turn the game around. He looked at the tailback and asked, "What's wrong?" The boy replied, "Coach, I can't run in these shoes." Coach told him to take them off. The team took the field and our tailback regained his old form. After he had scored our second touchdown, several teammates shed their shoes and tossed them toward the bench. We won the game.

Our tailback continued to play football in high school and became a star in basketball and track as well. During his junior year, he came to the attention of an opposing coach, who learned about his background and asked for an investigation. As it turned out, our star player couldn't confirm his age because he couldn't produce a birth certificate. That was grounds to challenge his eligibility. Gonzales' most prestigious law firm represented him in the case—but lost. The Interscholastic League declared him ineligible his senior year because of the maximum-age rule, which was nineteen. It broke his heart.

A local businessman took our tailback under his wing and arranged for him to play football at a nearby junior college while he finished his senior year of high school. At the time, he was six feet three inches tall and weighed only 155 pounds. He was grossly underweight because he had been so poorly fed. After three months of three square meals a day, he became an imposing 210-pounder. Four years later, he was named Little All American at a nearby college and earned a degree. He went on to have an outstanding career as a high school coach and administrator.

During all those years, I was responsible for finding my way home after practice. Many times I would hitchhike, making it as far as the Greenwood Road, and from there, I walked more than a mile to our house. On several occasions, I got a ride with a man who lived farther up the Greenwood Road. He worked in the chicken-processing plant in town. He got off work around 4:30 p.m. but never went directly home. He always stopped by the Los Amigos bar for a few cool ones. I waited for him in his 1940 pickup. Occasionally, he had more than a few. After a hot day in the processing plant, he developed a body odor that forced me to hug the door and hang my head out the window. He also liked to air out the engine in his pickup. What a frightening experience: speeding down Highway 90A at seventy-five miles an hour (or more) with a half-drunk driver. There seemed to be a direct correlation between the number of beers he had and the weight of his foot on the accelerator. Somehow, we always made it. When he would drop me off at the cattle guard, he enjoyed speeding away, throwing gravel under the rear fender and into the air. That was certainly a case of "the taillights looking a whole lot better than the headlights."

A couple of years later, in 1951, after we had won our first district championship in seven years, he approached me as I walked off the field. I was savoring success, hearing "great job" from the fans, and receiving congratulatory handshakes. He charged up to me, drunk as a skunk, and gave me a big bear hug. That stale-beer smell brought back memories. He slipped a five-dollar bill in the palm of my hand and shouted, "Nice game, Buddy. You won twenty-five dollars for me tonight!" Big money was changing hands, and "Friday night fever" was electrifying Gonzales.

I always had tremendous coaches. My ninth-grade coach used to say, "If you're going to win, you have to fight" and "Sacrifice your body—fight!" One night on the bus as we traveled home from a game, I jokingly asked him why he used the word "fight" so much. He said the only way to get what's really important is to fight for it. I later learned he was a fighter pilot in World War II who had been shot down and spent eighteen months in a German POW camp. Another member of the "Greatest Generation" served as my mentor.

A coach once told me I had to improve 900 percent before he would speak to me again. After I made the starting lineup, I asked about his cold-shoulder tactic. He said he had already picked me to be a starter but wanted me to improve. He knew how to motivate a Depression kid. And so did another coach my senior year. Alan Winters knew that families like mine had struggled through difficult times during the Depression. "Everything you have can be taken away from you," he would say, "but no one can take away your pride." It was a powerful motivator. We didn't win state that year, but we advanced further into the playoffs than any Apache team ever had in the past.

By the time I reached high school, football had become a family event. Sis, an Apache cheerleader, rallied the team from the sidelines. I'm definitely biased, but she was the prettiest, and she could jump the highest. Mom and Dad just beamed as they watched from the stands. They had become truly avid fans. They attended all my home games and most of the out-of-town ones. Regardless of where the game was played, they were always waiting for me at the high school afterward. They were anxious to get the full report. Mom had the first question: "Did you get hurt?" (I was lucky. I was often bruised and shook up but seldom injured.) Dad always asked, "How well do you think you did?" The question usually prompted me to truthfully assess my performance. He advised me to never be satisfied with my game. It was important to him how I handled victory as well as defeat.

In the last game of my junior year, my folks saw me get into a fight with the opposing team's nose guard. It happened after the last play of the game. I blew up because we had lost the game—and the district championship. We slugged it out as the fans converged on the field. Somebody finally separated us. It was the only time Dad ever criticized my "on-the-field" performance. I rationalized that I couldn't have drawn a penalty because the game was over. That provoked Dad: "It looked to me like you got a bad whippin'. I know it's hard to handle the short end of a butt-kicking, but if a man gets the best of you, you're going to have to deal with it better." He was right.

When we returned home after the game, Mom cooked some of her delicious sausage and eggs. While we ate, we continued to talk football until we wound down.

As "Friday night fever" became more infectious, football players and their families crossed socioeconomic boundaries. When a country boy or a poor kid succeeded on the gridiron, he and his family rose in status in the community. For my family and me, it was a gratifying experience. People we didn't even know spoke to us and called us by name. What a wonderful reward!

The Los Amigos bar has stood the test of time for over fifty-five years. After practice, I waited outside in the pickup for my ride.

Christmas and Miss Pearl

Christmas was always a church and family affair. As I remember it, the Christmas service of the First Evangelical Lutheran Church took place the Sunday before Christmas. The children acted out the story of Mary and Joseph finding no room at the inn and taking shelter in the stable. Mom helped direct the play a couple of times; I never got a role higher than a shepherd.

On Christmas Eve we went to Grandma Schrader's house to celebrate with the aunts, uncles and cousins on my father's side of the family. We would cut down a cedar tree in the woods, and all of us would decorate it. Some would thread popcorn on a string and loop it around the branches. Others would hang peppermint candy canes and tinsel icicles on the tree. For lights, we used clip-on wax candles. We also made bouquets of chaparral (desert hackberry) branches and stuck gumdrops on the thorns. At supper, the adults ate first, the table was cleared, and then the children ate. Baked turkey was the traditional entrée, and everybody brought a dish, usually whatever was produced on the farm. Then we gathered around the tree and lit the candles while Dad passed out gifts, usually apples and oranges, from the grandparents to the grandchildren. We would end the evening by popping firecrackers and lighting sparklers. (That was the only time of year we had fireworks; we never had them on the Fourth of July.)

On Christmas morning we stayed home and opened the few gifts we had under our tree. When I was about five, Brother told me there really was no Santa Claus, destroying my belief in the jolly old elf who would bring me presents if I were good. When Mom found out, she got really mad. But the cat was out of the bag. After that, I didn't listen for bells on the roof or jump out of bed to see what Santa had left under the tree. I just opened the one or two presents from Mom and Dad—and was grateful for those. One year, while we still lived on the Foster place, Brother got the best present of all—a second-hand bicycle from Uncle Olen and Aunt Agnes. That was a special Christmas. (I got a used bicycle several years later, but I paid for it myself with the five dollars I earned picking a neighbor's cotton for a week.)

After opening gifts, we went to Grandma and Grandpa Vackar's house to celebrate with Mom's side of the family. Again, this was a time to visit with cousins and share a meal together. These gatherings at Christmas were the only times I saw the men drink hard liquor. Each man was poured a shot and drank it straight. Mom always kept a sharp eye on Dad, supervising his consumption.

The Christmas that stands out most in my memory was 1947. On Christmas Eve afternoon, while Dad was on the courthouse square, the local Ford dealer approached him: "Would you be interested in a new 1948 Ford Deluxe?" What a question! Of course, he wanted it. We had been on the list since 1944, waiting for the war to end and automobile production to begin. Production did begin again in early 1946, but it took two years for the list to dwindle and our name to make it to the top.

Word spread quickly that we had bought a new car. The entire Schrader family congregated at the Ford dealership in a matter of minutes. Brother, home from Texas Tech, somehow got the word and immediately responded. It was a good thing because he had to drive the new vehicle. Dad was not familiar with the gearshift, which was on the steering-wheel column, so Brother had to give him a quick crash course. We drove around the courthouse square, sitting tall and waving as if we were in a parade. We tried to be humble and sophisticated, but the excitement was overwhelming.

Mom and Dad extended the celebration by motoring to Grandma and Grandpa Vackar's house on St. Vincent Street. Grandpa opened and closed the car door several times, checking to see "how tight it was built." I'm sure he kicked the tires. We were still excited that night at Grandma Schrader's annual Christmas Eve party. The new car, with all the exclamations, oohs and aahs, even upstaged the opening of the Christmas presents.

Our new jewel of an automobile was white, and Mom said it shined like a pearl. Sis suggested we call her Miss Pearl, and the name stuck. Miss Pearl had a push-button radio, a heater (we broke it in, and all of us broke out in a sweat), a big clock on the dash, and four windows that rolled up and down. After the 100-horsepower engine was broken in, we could travel in excess of thirty-five miles per hour. Once the break-in period had passed, Brother kicked it up to sixty miles per hour and announced that we were traveling at the rate of a mile a minute! I doubted that airplanes could travel that fast!

Miss Pearl had elevated our status in the community, and in turn had boosted the family's morale. The car we drove no longer made the statement that we were poor. In fact, we had moved a few rungs up the status ladder. For a short while, it was even fun going to church; we no longer parked at the far edge of the parking lot. Miss Pearl was in a class with the best in town.

The total drive-out cost of our new vehicle was $1,718.00, and every payment was no later than one week early. For the first year, Miss Pearl had a weekly bath—more frequently if it rained. During that time, we put at least three-eighths of an inch of Turtle Wax on her well-protected body. Dad said, "She's so slick, a fly can't land on her."

A week after getting Miss Pearl, on New Year's Day, Mom and Dad had a special dinner for the family. I knew it was special, because there were homemade cloth napkins on the table. It was a day of thanksgiving and a time to count our blessings. . . blessings from the good earth. During the first seven years of the 1940s, Mom and Dad reflected, we moved into a new home of our own with electricity and running water. We were enjoying a refrigerator and a butane-gas cookstove, and we had just bought our first tractor. (I'm not sure which was more gratifying: saying goodbye to the mules or saying goodbye to Blackie). We had a member of the family in college, and now we had Miss Pearl. Dad reminded us how all our hard work, teamwork and devotion to one another had paid off.

Dad's closing statement that day was the most inspirational message I can remember. In his gentle tone he said, "We are all proud of each other, we have our health, the Depression is behind us, and the greatest achievement is that our family will soon have a college graduate." Dad was looking me straight in the eye. The message was soft and subtle, but I heard it loud and clear. Sis and I got up and began doing the dishes. As always, she washed and I dried.

Blessings from the Good Earth

ORDER FORM

If you would like to order additional copies of *Blessings from the Good Earth*, fill out the form below. Please print.

____
Name

____
Street Address or P.O. Box

____

____
City State ZIP

____
Phone Fax E-mail

_______Check or money order is enclosed.

Quantity		Unit price	Shipping		Texas sales tax*	Total
_______	x	$17.95 +	$2.00	x	0.0625 =	$______

* Texas residents only. If you are not a Texas resident, do not pay sales tax. If you are exempt from Texas state sales tax, please provide documentation.

Make your check or money order payable to Buddy Schrader.
Please allow one to two weeks for delivery.

If you have questions, fax them to 1-830-596-0229.

Mail to:
The Good Earth Press
PO Box 9091
Horseshoe Bay, TX 78657